When things get back to normal

D1519419

M.T. DOHANEY

When things get back to normal

GOOSE LANE

Copyright © M.T. Dohaney, 1989, 2002.
Foreword © Helen Fogwill Porter, 2002.

All rights reserved. No part of this work may be reproduced or used in any form
or by any means, electronic or mechanical, including photocopying, recording, or any
retrieval system, without the prior written permission of the publisher. Any requests
for photocopying of any part of this book should be directed in writing to the
Canadian Copyright Licensing Agency.

When Things Get Back to Normal first published by Pottersfield Press, 1989. This
Trade edition published by Goose Lane Editions, 2002.

Cover photograph: Eyewire Inc.
Cover and book design by Julie Scriver.
Printed in Canada by Transcontinental Printing.
10   9   8   7   6   5   4   3   2   1

National Library of Canada Cataloguing in Publication Data

Dohaney, M.T., date
   When things get back to normal

2nd ed.
ISBN 0-86492-338-4

   1. Dohaney, M.T., date   2. Bereavement.
   3. Widows – Newfoundland – Biography.   I. Title.

HQ1058.5.C3D64 2002   155.9'37'092   C2002-900468-3

Published with the financial support of the Canada Council for the Arts, the
Government of Canada through the Book Publishing Industry Development
Program, and the New Brunswick Culture and Sports Secretariat.

Goose Lane Editions
469 King Street
Fredericton, New Brunswick
CANADA E3B 1E5

For Walt

*I wrote this journal for you and for me
and because my friend Anne said I should
put my sorrow into paper words.*

FOREWORD
Helen Fogwill Porter

In my youth I read every book ever written by Lucy Maud Montgomery. Even today, in what I like to call my oldth, I still reread them from time to time. As I prepared to write this foreword, I recalled an incident in *Anne of Avonlea*. One stormy day early in Anne Shirley's teaching career, she asks her students to tell her what they want more than anything else in the world. "To be a widow," says ten-year-old Marjory White. She claims that if you aren't married, people call you an old maid, and if you are, your husband bosses you around. If you're a widow, there is no danger of either.

In Dorothy Speak's recent novel *The Wife Tree*, a seventy-five-year-old woman named Morgan Hazzard describes the widows in her neighbourhood: "[T]hey're content to be released from cooking three square meals a day, from the smell of a man in their bedsheets. From *Hockey Night in Canada*, all the while enjoying their husbands' pensions." Harsh judgments, but perhaps true in some cases. I wonder about the bedsheets, though. Years ago an elderly widow told me she took her husband's unwashed undershirt to bed with her every night. After I was widowed myself, I understood the need for that physical reminder.

In *When Things Get Back to Normal*, M.T. (Jean) Dohaney has written a straightforward, moving account of her life in the year following the death of her husband, Walter. This book began as a journal. That's why there's such immediacy to every section of it. Walt died suddenly on November 22, 1986, after playing hockey. He was fifty-four. Less than a week later, Jean wrote these words: "I have been daughter, sister, wife, mother. These labels covered only part of me, yet increased all of me. 'Widow' covers all of me and decreases all of me. I learned yesterday that the word widow is derived from the Latin *viduus*, meaning empty."

I first picked up *When Things Get Back to Normal* a few years after my own husband, John, died suddenly of a massive heart attack at the age of fifty-three. I read it compulsively. Here at last was somebody who understood my situation perfectly. This was no cloying self-help guide that talked about God's will and a mystical eternal plan but a fearless summation of how it feels to lose the person you love most in the world.

"You're a widow now," my daughter Anne said to me shortly after John was pronounced dead. For some odd reason that bald statement helped me more than all the platitudes I'd be hearing over the next several days. People mean well but find it difficult to put their feelings into words and often resort to the tried and true. I've done the same thing myself. Anne's stark confirmation of my new status gave me a strange kind of comfort. As long as no one called me a relict! I'd had a horror of that word ever since I first read it in an L.M. Montgomery novel. In *A Tangled Web*, Aunt Betsy Dark, shortly before she died at eighty-five, announced that she was not to be called a relict. The dictionary defines relict as "a widow. Archaic." It makes me think of someone left over and useless. Apparently it was never used in reference to a man.

"The vultures are circling," reads Jean Dohaney's journal entry for December 3. "Will I be selling the house? . . . Am I interested in a monument? If I place an order before Christmas but agree not to have it installed until the frost goes out of the ground, I can take advantage of a special bonus: my name and age engraved for free." I remember a similar offer. The gentleman I talked to at Muir's Marble Works was more tactful. "You're a young woman," he said. (Was I? I was fifty-two.) "You could move away, make your home in another part of the world." He didn't say "marry again," though I sensed it was in his mind.

If he had coaxed me the other way, I might have given in. That was a vulnerable time for me. As it is, only my husband's name and dates appear on the simple marker I selected, along with the three words "Love Never Faileth." When I visit the cemetery now and read names and birth dates, with only the survivors' death dates to be filled in, I'm glad I resisted an early impulse to bring myself as close as possible to my own burial. Caitlin Thomas, the wife of the famous Welsh poet Dylan Thomas, wrote a book after he died. She called it *Leftover Life to Kill*. That title has meaning for many widows, especially in the early stages of grief. Caitlin was probably feeling like a relict, or a relic, when she chose it.

"My memory refuses to function," Jean says on December 10. "I miss appointments, mislay documents and forget house keys and car keys." I did all those things in the winter months after John died. I had never imagined that such mundane mishaps plagued people following bereavement. I had pictured widowhood as a sombre, grief-stricken time, but I had not foreseen the small, insistent irritations. I fell down a lot. Always a bit clumsy and uncoordinated, I had relied on John to keep me steady and would "link in" to him even if we were walking only a short distance. But it wasn't just my congenital awkwardness. My mind wouldn't stay on what I was doing. It had a life of its own. One night I tripped and fell flat on my face walking home from the corner store. For a while I looked almost as bruised on the surface as I felt inside.

In May, "the merriest month of all the year," Jean ran into an acquaintance she had not seen since Walt's death. After offering her condolences, this well-meaning woman uttered the words Jean had been dreading — "Life goes on." "I wanted to shout at her," Jean wrote that day. "Maybe it does for you, but not for me." Instead she replied, "So they tell me." For a few weeks after John died, I hated meeting people who would feel that they had to express sympathy, or, worse still, who had missed the news of John's death and asked about him as if he were waiting for me nearby. At times, going to a shopping centre with my daughters, I would stay in the car alone while they did my errands. Where was that gregarious woman my younger relatives had labelled "Step, step, chat"? At the same time, I welcomed friends and relatives who came to visit, especially at night. They knew that just being there with me, drinking tea, was enough. Near the end of her first year of widowhood, Jean says, "I couldn't have trudged the path without the constancy of friends." I dread to think of bereaved people who don't have that kind of support.

"But Jean, you're strong." These were words Jean heard far too often. "They say this as though hard knocks don't give me pain. I want to shout at them, 'I'm not strong. I'm weak. I'm a pathetic creature. I hurt all over.'" My Grandmother Horwood used to say, "God fits the back for the burden." We hear that kind of thing when a woman gives birth to an incredibly damaged child or someone suffers an unbelievable loss. "I'd never be able to handle it," I once heard a friend say. "God must give extra strength to people who have to bear something like that." I bit my tongue when I heard this. I lost my father, my younger brother, and my husband to sudden death within eleven months. My wish is that God had given me a weaker back and fewer burdens.

Nine months after her husband's death, Jean was walking across the university campus in Fredericton when an indescribable sadness enveloped her. She ordered herself to think of "something, anything" that could bring a little joy into her life. Among other decadent notions, she came up with the idea of having "an affair! A short but blazing affair." She soon realized she couldn't think of anyone to have an affair with. "Besides," she asked herself, "where would I get the energy to go out and buy new lingerie?" Immediately after John's death, a friend's husband assured her that I'd marry again within the year. He was wrong. Like Jean, I'm still single. As a popular country song has it, "I'm not that lonely yet."

Toward the end of her journal and the year, Jean made up a set of rules for herself. One of them was, "Warm my own feet." Right after John died, I began bringing a hot water bottle upstairs with me every night. The wide bed that I'd slept in with John for nearly thirty years could be awfully cold with only one body in it. And my big black cat Smudge knew enough to sprawl across my feet. The sex act is given such high priority in today's world that we often forget the sheer bliss that comes from two bodies lying entwined. I know of several bereaved people who have rushed into new physical relationships simply because they couldn't stand sleeping alone. I didn't take that road, and neither did Jean, but we understand those who do.

I first read *When Things Get Back to Normal* after I became a widow, but that doesn't mean it can't be appreciated by someone who's still part of a couple. This book has clarity, compassion, humour and, above all, honesty. It's a fact of life that a majority of us women will end up on our own.

Things don't ever really "get back to normal" after the death of a spouse. If we're lucky, we find a new kind of normal that is made bearable by memories, good friends and relatives, involvement with others and a strong sense of self.

Give sorrow words. The grief that does not speak
Whispers o'er fraught heart and bids it break.

– Macbeth

This morning for a split second my life was back to normal. The radio alarm on your side of our king-size bed jolted me out of an exhausted sleep, and in that haze of half awake, I forgot you had died. I reached out to pull you close. My hand groped for your warm body and found only unrumpled sheets, cool against the flesh.

I'm told I should be thankful you went in your health, so to speak, having skated your heart out at hockey. But like Hamlet, beggar that I am, I am even poor in thanks. I feel nothing. Not gratitude. Not anger. Not sorrow. I stagger through the days stunned by the swiftness with which my life has emptied.

You left the house on Friday evening, invincible in shoulder pads and shin guards. When I saw you again, death had reduced you to the navy blue suit you kept for sedate occasions. I'm certain that, if you had had any say in the matter, you would have worn your paint-splattered jeans and your T-shirt with the threadbare elbows. My fingers ached to loosen your tie and let your shirt collar gape open.

As my mother would have said, you had a lovely funeral, and I thought it a pity you couldn't have witnessed the packed church. I'm told there was standing room only. Even the choir loft was filled.

On the drive to the church, I saw people going on with their lives just as if the world hadn't stopped. A young man wearing a radio headset stood on the sidewalk and absently watched the procession as he waited for the light to turn green. His arms kept time to the music that flooded his ears.

I was so certain you'd be home by the time I returned from the service that I filed away bits of information I thought you'd enjoy: for example, how Steven, without my knowledge, smuggled your hockey stick to the cemetery and dropped it into your grave so you would have something familiar waiting for you there.

I started searching the crowd for you the minute I got back to the house. I was so tired. So woebegone. I wished I could find a private corner where I could crouch into a ball and keen my misery away. But how could I escape when I had a houseful of guests and you hadn't shown up to take over?

As time passed and there was still no sign of you, I began to get angry. What was keeping you? How could you expect me to wake you, bury you and be a hostess as well? I wandered aimlessly through the crowd, making robotic conversation here and there, and feeling I should be apologizing for your absence. Even as I passed the sandwiches and replenished the tea, I kept an ear cocked for your footsteps on the back veranda.

A woman remarked as she picked up a watercress sandwich that President Kennedy also died on November 22. That night, when I lay wide awake in bed, I wondered how Mrs. Kennedy had felt on her first "after the burial" night. Did she substitute her pillow for his, hoping it would make the bed less lonely? Did she want to get dressed and go to the cemetery to keep him company in case he felt abandoned and lonely, surrounded as he was by strangers – dead strangers? Did she herself feel abandoned, the relatives and friends having gone back to their own lives and the fever of the last few days suddenly no more? And later, as the weeks and months passed, did she search the calendar for that significant date, saying, as my mother had said, her voice far away. "This day last month he was still here." And still later, "This day last year. . . . "

NOVEMBER 29 – *Friday*

I was called a widow today. "Sign here," the girl in the office of vital statistics said when I went to pick up a copy of your death certificate. She pointed with a geranium-red fingernail to indicate the spot she had Xed for my signature. "Right here. In the block that says widow of the deceased." The word pierced me like a lance, and my sharp intake of breath was audible even though the office was noisy with others seeking proof of beginnings and endings.

Later, as I walked home, I tried to give voice to my new label. *Widow! Widow!* I mouthed the word over and over, and although I could hear it thundering in my soul, no sound would leave my lips. The letters bunched up on my tongue and clung there like soot to a chimney. Until two weeks ago, widow was only a word in the English language. Now it was me — a woman with a life as bleak as that sky on the day we lowered you into the half frozen November ground. I have been daughter, sister, wife, mother. These labels covered only part of me, yet increased all of me. Widow covers all of me and decreases all of me. I learned yesterday that the word widow is derived from the Latin *viduus*, meaning empty.

DECEMBER 2 – *Monday*

Went back to work today. Farewell sabbatical leave! Walking in through those university gates alone, when for the past fifteen years we had gone together, took an act of strength I was convinced I didn't have. (Yes, I said walking. You predicted correctly. The day did come when I wished I hadn't turned the driving over to you.) When I got to my office, I closed the door (I wasn't up to condolences) and attacked the piled-up assignments. I think I was lenient with my red pencil. What, I reasoned, signified a pass or a fail in technical writing when, with the swiftness of a pen-stroke, some higher force could snuff out a life? Maybe later such things as standards of excellence will once again be important to me.

I'm told that going back to work is the best medicine

for "taking my mind off it all." People say this with such conviction that I'm sure they believe it. Don't they understand that nothing – absolutely nothing – can divert my thoughts? The pockets of my mind and heart and soul are bloated with pain. The trouble with grief is that it can't be viewed. If my arms were newly severed, would anyone suggest that I go to work to take my mind off my loss? My friend L. said she wished people could have a barometer in their foreheads for measuring pain of the heart. If others could see the extent of your suffering, they wouldn't be so quick to ply you with platitudes.

DECEMBER 3 – *Tuesday*

They say I'm taking it well. They mean your death, of course, even though they can't bring themselves to voice the word. I've cancelled your credit cards. I even registered the envelopes bulging with chopped-up plastic. I gathered your belongings into piles: to be thrown away, to be given to charity, to be passed on for memories – diamond ring, gold cuff links, new tuxedo, never worn, an anniversary gift from me in October when I still had expectations of a long and full social life. I know what I'm about to say is a cliché, and you know how I hate clichés, but it is so true that old habits hang tough. Before I threw your cast-offs into the green garbage bag, I got the scissors to snip the buttons from your shirts. I actually had a couple in my hand before I realized what I was doing. It was a really low moment when I came to grips with the fact that I no longer have any need to save shirt buttons. My sewing box already has a quart bottle filled to the top with small, white pearlized buttons, and, unless I intend to open a button factory, I now have enough shirt buttons to last a lifetime, however long or short that may be.

But if I'm taking your death so well, why do I feel like Dorothy in *The Wizard of Oz*? I feel as if I've been scooped up by a tornado and spiralled into another dimension, where nothing is as it was or as it should be.

I have taken on the responsibility for the details of your life at a time when I can barely cope with the details of my own. Every day the list lengthens. Get the death certificate. Send in the insurance forms. Cancel memberships here and there. Close out bank accounts. Clear out safety deposit box. Change over Medicare coverage. Change car registration. Let this one and that one know you won't be chairing a meeting, attending a conference, giving a paper. While I try to get these things looked after, the thank-you notes for mass cards, letters of sympathy, flowers, food and donations to your scholarship fund lie fallow on the coffee table in the front room.

Then too, the vultures are circling. Will I be selling the house? Lawnmower? Snowblower? Tools? Am I interested in a monument? If I place an order for a monument before Christmas but agree not to have it installed until the frost goes out of the ground, I can take advantage of a special bonus: my name and age engraved for free. Imagine! Me, a chronic falsifier of natal date, making a public proclamation of it on a slab of marble.

Yesterday I was made an offer I couldn't refuse. Only I did. If I will order fifty four-by-five-inch laminated copies of your obituary notice, I can have the lot for the same price as the two-by-two size. Now what use would I have for fifty laminated obituary notices? It isn't the sort of thing you'd display on your coffee table, is it?

DECEMBER 4 – *Wednesday*

I broke the lease on the Arizona apartment today. Man proposes, God disposes. We had planned our sabbatical year so carefully: a novel for me, a textbook for you, and all of that sunshine, not to mention our first release from domestic responsibility in thirty years. I used to lie in bed and happily anticipate the coming months. On the night of November 21 I told myself that nirvana was only five weeks, two final examinations and seven hockey games away.

It is difficult to believe that your life petered out while I placidly watched the "doings of the Ewings" on television. Surely the earth should have trembled to presage such a terrible event!

When the doctor told me you were dead, I didn't believe him. At any moment I was certain you were going to burst into that room at the hospital they euphemistically call "the quiet room" and announce you were ready to go home. I was even prepared to be embarrassed by your wet-with-perspiration uniform, especially with that battle-scarred sweater. But you didn't come to me, and later, at home, I lay on our bed and waited well into the night for the call that would announce you had been revived.

How could you be dead? You were never sick in your life. You'd get a touch of a headache, a touch of the flu. Surely what you had suffered at the rink was only a touch of a heart attack. But as the night wore on and friends and relatives came, I knew you were gone — permanently gone — and it was as though someone had dropped a wet tarpaulin over my head and smothered the life out of me as well. In those very early moments, I could feel the loneliness of the years ahead.

I huddled on top of the bedspread, drew my legs up towards my chin and let the night slide into morning.

DECEMBER 6 – *Friday*

I don't know which is the more difficult to do — leave this house or return to it after I've been away for a few hours. When I am inside its walls I feel safe, but once I go out the door I become vulnerable, my wounds uncovered. I cringe as if a thousand arrows are waiting to jab at my naked self.

When I return home, even if after only a brief absence, the silence of the house assaults me. One night last week, I slept at a friend's house. I came back before the neighbourhood had wakened up. How still the rooms were! Even the refrigerator with that ever-running motor was silent. The reality of your death and the rawness of my widowhood made me sick to my stomach.

DECEMBER 7 – *Saturday*

Two weeks plus a day since you died and the first weekend without you. This is not technically correct, but the other two weekends, like the weekdays, went by in a blur of disbelief and horror. I am conscious of today. I am conscious of being lonely.

We had our first snowfall last night. A really big one. I spent the morning shovelling the driveway. I forgot to put your car in the garage so I had to broom the snow off it as well. I raged at you with every swipe. Why did you have to skate yourself to death? Why did you have to die in the winter? Surely you, above everyone else, knew how much I hate winter.

Once I had the cleaned-off car moved into the garage, I attacked the driveway. I must have looked a pathetic sight, wielding that big shovel of yours, because our neighbours' boy came over to help. I worked along with him, although I wanted to pitch the shovel in a snow bank and come in where it was warm. When I finally did come in, my hands and feet were so numb I had to sit in a bathtub and let warm water thaw my flesh. I wondered if warm water would thaw out a numbed heart.

DECEMBER 8 – *Sunday*

I'm sitting at the kitchen table, staring at your empty chair while sounds of the neighbours leaving for church filter in through the clapboards.

I miss you so much even my hair hurts. Your death has blinded my eyes to beauty. Do you know I can no longer see in colour – just black and grey?

I stood before the bathroom mirror this morning and sized up my reflection. It's the first time since the funeral that I have given more than a hurried thought to my appearance. I'm sure there must have been many days during the last couple of weeks when I looked as un-kempt as if I had spent the night under newspapers on a sidewalk grating. The person who looked back at me from the mirror was a stranger. She had a stupefied look. I was reminded of a cat I had as a child. She liked to sleep in the rocking chair by the fire. We all respected her wish – all except Grandfather. He would come in and, with a scoop of his hand, land her on the floor. She would stand there blinking in confusion, a dazed "what happened?" look on her face.

DECEMBER 10 – *Tuesday*

The weight of my grief has slowed me down almost to a stop. My friends say I should seek therapy, but I say I have a right to this grief and don't want to pay big dollars to have it lifted from my shoulders. In the words of Richard II, *You may my glories and my state depose, But not my griefs; still am I king of those*. Maybe some people would call this wallowing, but I call it survival.

My memory refuses to function. I miss appointments, mislay documents and forget house keys, car keys, office keys, as well as leave behind umbrellas, gloves, scarves, purses and whatever else of my personal belongings that can come loose. I'm forever jimmying our porch door open, and the secretary at work has threatened to tape my office key to my wrist.

I even forget to buy food. Not that eating forms a big part of my life. I'm really into comfort food, though: ice cream, bread, yogurt, chocolate. Already my waist is beginning to expand. But ask me if I care. Two questions consume me. How can I continue without you? How can I spend a winter alone in this house, scared as I am of things that go bump in the night?

People keep coming up to me and saying, "I'm sorry you *lost* Walt." I know they use this word because they can't bring themselves to use any part of the verb "to die." Still, I come away feeling that I've misplaced you, along with my other belongings. Careless Jean has lost her umbrella and her husband. And all within the space of a few weeks.

DECEMBER 12 – *Thursday*

The contents of your office arrived today. I felt like a voyeur going through your cancelled cheques, copies of notices to students, reminders to self, receipts for donations and memberships, etc. As I sorted out the remnants of your life, I had a perverse wish to uncover a secret life – a short tryst, a lengthy affair, a few stolen moments. The anger over your deception would have been a welcome respite from the pain that now saturates me.

I found no such evidence, though, and, as a matter of fact, the innocent accumulation of material just made me more aware of how special you were. Do you know that some evenings when I'm approaching the house, tired from work, I get angry because you were such an affable human being? I think that if you had been a difficult person to live with, I could cope a lot better with returning to the empty house. Is this crazy thinking or isn't this crazy thinking? Maybe I do need therapy. Maybe I am going over the edge.

People think they can make me feel better by telling me about others who have had harder blows than mine. They don't seem to understand that at this time I have no capacity for dealing in degrees of pain, and because I am expending all of my emotions on myself, I have none left over for the hardships of my neighbour.

My soul is dead and my heart is overflowing with emptiness.

I can't seem to cope with the neverness of death. Will I never again feel your arms around me? Never? Will I never again hear your laugh? Never? Will I never again watch you getting dressed and pulling your partly buttoned shirt over your head because it's quicker to get it on that way?

Sometimes I catch myself playing "let's pretend." I look at the picture of us that is hanging in the dining room – the whole smiling family – and I make believe the children are small again, and at any moment you will come striding in from work and scoop us up in your arms. I save this game for especially terrible times because it is scary how tempting it is to permanently slip into a place where the ugliness of reality doesn't exist.

DECEMBER 14 – *Saturday*

Today I was walking downtown, and I saw someone I knew walking along on the opposite side of the street. He waved a cheery hello, and I returned his wave, equally cheerily, even though I had just mopped away the tears that, seconds earlier, had streamed down my face, unbidden and unannounced. Afterwards, I wondered about the number of people who go about their day waving cheerily while their hearts are weighted with sorrow. Thoreau was probably right when he said most of us lead lives of quiet desperation.

Later on during that walk, I came face to face with someone who made it impossible for me even to force a cheerful exterior. She wanted to know the gory details. Did you die on the ice, in the dressing room or in the ambulance? Were you in the shower? Were you still dressed in your hockey equipment? I wanted to be mischievous and say you almost never took a shower in your hockey equipment because water plays havoc with shin guards, but I couldn't manage that much levity, especially when she added consolingly, "But Jean, you have so much going for you. You'll be remarried in no time at all." She predicted on the outskirts of a year. I said when my cat got run over by a car I waited longer than that to get another one. She nodded without the slightest understanding. "That's the trouble with cats," she said. "They get themselves killed."

I've slowed down almost to a stop. I used to be such a mover and shaker that I practically met myself on the way to going somewhere else. Now it takes me a full hour to get dressed, a feat I could once accomplish in twenty minutes, fifteen if pressed. Some mornings are worse than others, and I've often used up two hours with nothing to show for the wasted time except washed teeth and combed hair and the books and papers I have to take back to the office humped into a pile by the front door. I'm told this slowness is a sign of depression. If that's the case, I must really be in the depths.

DECEMBER 16 – *Monday*

Thank God for good friends. They let me lean into them when I can no longer stand upright. We had three categories of friends: yours, mine and ours. In the beginning, all three were on hand. Now the group has withered down to a few of ours and a lot of mine. Mine are mostly women. Over the years they have enriched my life, and now they are sustaining it.

They have the sensitivity not to tell me that I must get on with my life. They know that, for now at least, I have no life, nor do I want one. Acquaintances are not so sensitive. "Life goes on," they say, as if I am malingering and it is now time I was up and about. Perhaps they say it because they think it is something I want to hear or to confirm that, for them at least, life does go on. Or perhaps it is as Shakespeare said, everyone can master a grief but he who has it.

DECEMBER 17 – *Tuesday*

Is there sleep after the death of a spouse? I walk myself into exhaustion every evening and yet sleep that knits up the ravelled sleeve of care eludes me. Maybe Macbeth was right – only the innocent sleep. I am tortured with guilt over my sins of commission and omission. I won't allow myself to recall the happy times. Instead I dwell on the things I said which I shouldn't have said, or on the things I should have said and didn't. I can't think of any short-comings of yours. When I telephoned our friend Al in Arizona and mentioned this to him, he said he can't wait to die so M. will canonize him. Is that what I'm doing to you?

What gives me the worst case of the guilts – positively the worst case – is that I can't recall you. I mean I can't recall the details of you. I try to picture you mowing the lawn, shovelling the walk, sitting at your desk grading exams, hunkered in your chair watching sports on television, and on and on, but no pictures come to mind. All that remains is the knowledge that you did do these things.

But now ask me to describe you in that casket and I

will supply you with the most minute detail. I can even see the rust stain on your little finger, just underneath your engineer's iron ring. I try to change the channel, but the same picture returns over and over again. It is as though the horror of you lying inert on that cold pleated satin has choked the life out of all other memories.

DECEMBER 18 – *Wednesday*

I've discovered there's nothing romantic about a sunrise if you have spent the dark hours roaming through empty rooms hoping daybreak will come before its time. Are insomnia and widowhood synonymous?

DECEMBER 19 – *Thursday*

The days trudge towards Christmas. Yesterday I suggested to the children that we go to a restaurant for dinner on Christmas Day. They wouldn't have been more shocked if I had suggested we peddle pornography on a street corner. Only those to be pitied, they said, eat in restaurants on Christmas Day.

It isn't easy for them, either. They remember other Christmases – the stairs garlanded in red and green, the fireplace burning brightly and friends and relatives seated at a laden table.

I'm certain the three of us would prefer to wake up one morning and discover we had slept through the twenty-fifth. I have learned a truth that my friend A. knew all along: special holidays make happy people happier and sad people sadder, and the more special the holiday, the more terrible it is for those who have no reason to celebrate it.

Christmas Eve

Haven't entered any thoughts for days. But then I haven't done much of anything for days. Heartache is consuming me.

This is the first Christmas Eve since we met that we will not be in church together. Isn't that an amazing record of togetherness? Steve came home last night for three days. We are going to early service. Although we haven't discussed it, neither of us is up to Midnight Mass. I hope the sermon doesn't dwell on the family aspect of Christmas.

Christmas Day

Morning has broken. It's finally here. Dreading its arrival didn't hold it back for an instant. Steve and I are sleeping late – or, more precisely, we are clinging late to the bed. Neither of us has even turned on our radio, knowing the Christmas music will pierce deep into our flesh.

Hallelujah the night! We went to the hotel for dinner. The four of us – Sue, Ben, Steve and I – were so very polite to each other. Ben was on his best behaviour and acted more like thirty-nine than nine. On the way home we confessed our relief that the dining room had been crowded and we hadn't felt like waifs in a storm. We came back to the house and gave Ben the gifts you had bought for him early in November. After he opened them, he said shyly that he dreamed about you last night. He saw you smiling down at him from Heaven. Were you?

Already I'm dreading next Christmas. Does time really heal? I wish I could believe it does.

Tonight I'm remembering other Christmases. I remember when you were an engineering student and Susan was just an infant. We had an attic apartment, and the roof was so slanted the only place you could stand up straight was in the centre of the living room. On Christmas Eve, after we put Susan to bed, we went out to the back veranda and reeled in the day's diapers. We had to crack them off the line. We brought them in and stood them over the heating ducts in the kitchen to thaw, and after a few minutes they leaned against the wall like tired old men. That night the sky was so blue it made the snow look blue, too. I have no idea why this memory has stayed with me all these years, but to this day, whenever I smell clean cotton drying, I recall that Christmas Eve.

Another special Christmas was the first one we spent in Arizona, when you were working on your doctorate. Alan was visiting us, and on Christmas Eve he played a record of Mel Torme singing "The Christmas Song." I got so lonely for home, especially when he sang that part about chestnuts roasting on an open fire, that I began to cry and Alan chided me, saying we never even had a fireplace at home, much less roasted chestnuts over one, so why the nostalgia? A little later we took the children for a drive in the desert, and we brought back a scraggly mesquite bush and decorated it with cookies because we were too poor to buy proper decorations. In the morning, Alan scoured our housing area for other displaced persons like ourselves. He found eight, and we had a delightful blueberry pancake breakfast.

Lately I've been thinking a lot about death. I need to believe in the existence of a hereafter. I mean I always believed, but now it is essential that I believe. I want to be able to rejoin you and Alan and the significant others who have left me behind. John Keats said, "life is but a day; a fragile dewdrop on its perilous way." For my part, I want life to be only an anteroom in that mansion of many rooms.

Actually, I'm now so preoccupied with death that I'm getting to be as bad as my mother, who, after my father's too-early death, wanted only to read the obituary notices in the newspaper. "Give me the section with the deaths," she would say in her heavy Irish brogue. Now I, too, am searching that column for signs of others dying before their time. I think it gives me comfort when I find I'm not the only one who has had someone suddenly snatched away. Macabre, yes!

DECEMBER 30 — *Monday*

Tomorrow is New Year's Eve, and I've decided to run away. Steve has gone back to work, and the house is like a tomb. Our friends F. & C. are insisting that I join them for our regular New Year's party. How can I sing "Auld Lang Syne" without your arm around my waist? Besides, my presence would probably put a pall on the party. I've decided to visit my friend B. in Ottawa. Going away without you will be a traumatic first, but surely it won't be as bad as staying here without you.

New Year's Eve — Ottawa

It is 12:30, so it is really New Year's Day. B. and I went to a movie — *Out of Africa*.

A song in the movie was one that was played at our wedding reception, "Let the Rest of the World Go By." I almost came unglued but kept my composure by devouring the economy-sized container of buttered popcorn B. bought in the lobby. She said it was to be our moment of decadence and the devil with spreading hips. We went to bed as soon as we returned to her apartment, neither of us wanting to wait for the New Year countdown on television or witness the rounds of merry kissing. We didn't even wish each other Happy New Year. I guess we sensed they would be empty words for both of us.

JANUARY 3, 1987 – *Friday*

I'm still in Ottawa. Went shopping today to pass the time while B. was at work. The first window display I came upon had a mannequin dressed in an overcoat identical to the one I gave you for your birthday last February. I said it made you look European, and you wanted to know what was wrong with looking Canadian. When I saw that coat in the window, I, a hardcore shopper, caved in. I lost all interest in the stores. Will my world always be as flat and as joyless as it is now?

JANUARY 5 – *Sunday*

Home again, home again . . . I haven't words to describe the loneliness of arriving at the airport last night without anyone to meet me and then having to come back to this house alone. I took a taxi from the airport, and anger at you got me inside the house. I was angry at you for dying and leaving me in such a mess.

My fury pumped up such adrenalin that I got the courage to search the basement for intruders, all the while praying to God I wouldn't find any. I blamed you for taking the joy out of returning to my well-ordered home. I always delighted in returning to this house after a hiatus. I especially loved my many-windowed kitchen. I could sit for hours and watch the sun filter in through the melon-coloured curtains and then slant across the green and white couches. Even in the midst of winter, there was a feeling of a hazy summer day.

JANUARY 6 – *Monday*

My friend A. came to visit me tonight. She chastized me for not letting her know when I was returning because she wanted to meet me at the airport. In a mellow mood after a couple of glasses of Bailey's Irish Cream, I confided to her that I am considering becoming a missionary. I explained that I now have this overpowering need to immerse myself in a great cause. "A missionary?" she hooted, waving her empty glass in my direction. "*You*? A missionary?" She leaned close to me as though she were going to impart a great secret and said in a very earnest voice, "Jean, you are the god-damnedest most self-indulgent woman I have ever known," and without further preamble she launched into the reasons why I am singularly unsuited to tracking down pagans in the bowels of Africa. She demanded to know how I am going to survive in the jungles and deserts without my foaming baths, my satin lingerie and my designer perfume. Then she, a confirmed atheist, asked how I could be so arrogant as to presume the Lord would choose me to do great deeds in far away places?

She's right, of course. I was being presumptuous. And I certainly do like my material comforts. Actually, I was thinking more along the lines of having a Popemobile shuttle me back to the Holiday Inn at the end of a hard day on the missionary hustings. I guess my spirit wants to minister to the needy in foreign lands, but my flesh wants pigskin gloves and wine in crystal goblets. A. said I should concentrate on what I do best — my writing.

I wonder if she's right. Will writing give me the centre I now crave?

JANUARY 9 – *Thursday*

My body, my heart and my soul ache for things to return to normal. I find peace nowhere. I find comfort nowhere. I find stability nowhere. I think of myself as walking endlessly on a winter plain, my feet and hands numbed from the frost, my heart searching for a shelter I know no longer exists. I want someone to be at the end of the journey to feed me warm soup and gently remove the boots from my swollen feet. But there is no one waiting at the journey's end. Indeed, there is no journey's end.

A recent acquaintance, whom I met because of our mutual newly widowed state, said she needed her husband for an anchor. I need you for a harbour. Are we saying the same thing, or is there a difference?

JANUARY 10 – *Friday*

The bathroom leaked through the ceiling this morning, and the clothes dryer won't heat. Worst of all, the lights in the driveway shorted last night on account of the heavy frost, and I'm told I can't get them fixed until spring. How I hate the responsibility of keeping a house in running order! Did you hate it also? Say no. It would lessen my guilt if you would say it didn't bother you at all.

Speaking of guilt. The two saddest words in the English dictionary have to be "if only." If only . . . if only . . . you've no idea how often in the course of a day, or, more aptly, in the course of a night, I whisper these words. If only I had been more insistent that you quit hockey, get a physical, take life easier. If only I had more fully appreciated your contribution to the quality and quantity of my life.

Still, I have a lot for which to be grateful. We truly were each other's best friend. The other day, someone commenting on our closeness said we were two halves joined as one. Actually, I'd say we were two wholes joined together to make a larger whole.

My mother and father were married friends. I remember a day when my father was out of work and job hunting. My mother and I were looking out the window, awaiting his return. Finally we saw him come trudging up the laneway. His jacket was slung over his shoulder, and he was gripping the neck of it as though that were the only thing keeping him upright. My mother sighed and whispered, more to herself than to me, "The poor devil, I hope he found work. For *his* sake." I'm certain I never managed that much selflessness.

JANUARY 11 – *Saturday*

Last night I couldn't sleep, but that in itself is nothing new. I walked the floor as usual and then about three a.m. I went into Steven's clothes closet. (He still hoards some of your clothes – but in his room at our house. There isn't enough space in his small apartment.) I took out a brown linen sports jacket of yours. I wrapped it around myself and curled up in fetal position on your side of the bed. When I woke up, the sun was high in the sky, or as high as it gets here at this time of year.

JANUARY 12 – *Sunday*

Another Sunday. They pile one upon another relentlessly. I'm just recovering from the loneliness of one when it's Friday night all over again. I often think of the old woman who came to the funeral parlour to pay her respects, although she had never met you – or, for that matter, us. "I didn't know the mister," she apologized. "It's just that I live near here and Sundays are so long." Her empty eyes still haunt me. Will I ever become so lonely I'll take to browsing in funeral parlours to while away a long Sunday afternoon?

A bit of good news. A female graduate student is going to move in with me for the winter. The cheap lodging will help her, and her company will make this big house less terrifying. By the time May rolls around, I should be able to come to a decision regarding whether to sell or not to sell.

What do I do with the rest of my life? Who will care about me or for me if I get sick? Who will find me if I trip on the stairs and kill myself? I certainly don't want the children to unlock the front door some day, annoyed because I won't answer my phone, and there on the carpet at the foot of the stairs they'll find me, sprawled out as though I've been dropped from a helicopter. How ignominious! Especially if I'm naked. Especially if several days have elapsed.

Yesterday, a recent divorcee told me that she missed the

institution of marriage more than she missed him. How I envied her. If I just missed marriage, I'd be putting my name in the personals for a husband replacement.

I'm having phantom sightings of you. I hear your steps on the stairs as you come to bed, having stayed up late to watch a hockey game. The steps creak under your weight. At the end of the working day, I hear you coming up my office corridor to collect me for the ride home. Sometimes I actually pull my chair back from my desk, making ready to leave. When it hits me that my mind is playing games, my stomach sinks.

JANUARY 13 – *Monday*

Bittersweet news. *The Corrigan Women* is going to be published. The Lord giveth and the Lord taketh. I sure hope He (She) doesn't believe that your death in exchange for the publication of my novel is a fair exchange. What is the good of happy news if I can't share it with you? Still, I do feel a flicker of something akin to delight or excitement. Maybe I'm not totally dead inside.

JANUARY 19 – *Sunday*

I'm really sad this morning. *Really* sad. It seems as though all of the progress I've made so far has disappeared.

Maybe, though, this dip into melancholy is the result of emotional growth. I'm beginning to accept your death – or accept the fact of your death. I no longer get jolted by the unrumpled pillow, and I no longer look for your car in the driveway when I come home from work. But there are aspects I can't accept. Will you never again rub your beard over my cheek, hug my body, ruffle my hair, hold my hand or warm my feet?

I'm still furious with God for snatching you from me, but I'm making moves toward reconciliation. I don't want you being held responsible for the sins of your wife. Still, every time I see a couple, even if they are engaged in something as mundane as picking up groceries, I have to stifle an inner rage. But in the beginning, I didn't stifle it. I would go home and storm through the house belligerently, asking, "Why! Why! Why!"

JANUARY 20 – *Monday*

Will January ever end?

My housemate has moved in, and while she's considerably younger than me, the age difference disappears over a cup of coffee and an exchange of hurts. She, too, is working her way through a sorrow.

I walked to work today. It was thirty below zero. That's taking the wind chill factor into account. All the way there I cried behind my big woollen scarf. By the time I arrived, my eyelids were dripping icicles. I closed my door and cried and cried and cried. I cried for the frustration and inconvenience of my life and for my cowardice in not driving the car.

I picked up groceries this evening. I dread this chore because I'm embarrassed by the few items in my cart.

I hurt all over when I see full carts. A full cart, a full life. Right? I go to great lengths to hide my singleness from the store clerks. For example, I buy more meat than I need because I don't want the man at the meat counter to detect my solitary existence. I don't want him to feel sorry for me and patronize me like I've often heard butchers patronize their customers: "Here you are, dear, a quarter pound of hamburger and four sausages." I also dread meeting acquaintances in the aisles. I notice them glancing in my cart to see what I'm eating these days. I think they expect to find toast and tea — the staples of the lonely.

JANUARY 22 — *Wednesday*

I met an old acquaintance yesterday. He's in the radio business — program director, I think he said. He told me he will help me get on *Morningside* when my book comes out.

How I ached to rush back and tell you this news.

My friend L. came over last night. We talked about new beginnings — hers, not mine. She wondered whether she will ever again trust a man. I guess it isn't easy to move beyond betrayal.

There was a beautiful sunset this evening, but without you it meant only the end of a lonely day and the beginning of a lonely night.

JANUARY 23 – *Thursday*

I have made a pact with myself. Before spring arrives, I'm going to wake up one morning and my second thought will be, He's dead. I can't imagine what my first thought will be, but it will have to be something very special.

JANUARY 28 – *Tuesday*

The house adjoining our lot at the back always has a light burning in the hall window. A widow's house. Over the years, when I would notice this light I always whispered, "Please God, don't make it necessary for me to light up a room to keep the dark at bay." Now at this very moment my hall light is casting a yellow shadow over the concrete slabs in our driveway.

FEBRUARY – *Groundhog Day*

The children phoned. We talked about inconsequential things. Perhaps next year we'll be able to say, "This is Dad's birthday."

Several people from your department have asked me to supper, but I have always declined. I'm bone weary, emotionally and physically, and I don't have any energy to expend on conversation, particularly on conversation which studiously avoids the subject of you. Besides, it is very draining to be around couples with whom we used to socialize.

FEBRUARY 7 – *Friday*

A. and I went to a restaurant. We go every Friday night. We talk and talk and talk. I don't think I could get through the week without this night in the offing.

Several pieces of mail arrived for you today. What pain it causes me when I have to readdress an envelope and check off "deceased" in the box marked "reason for return." Another pain-filled piece of mail is the letter that is addressed to "the estate of. . . ." Death isn't buried in the cemetery on the day of the funeral. You have to keep burying it over and over again.

My energy level is still batting zero. I rarely clean the house. I, a typical Virgo, organized and neat to the point of fault, have become almost slovenly. Sometimes when I go to my office and see the piles of assignments lying ungraded, I want to pick them up and in a frenzy scatter them helter skelter around the room like a mad scientist.

Lately I've been flirting with the idea of taking flight from reality. I'm so tired. All of my energy goes into staving off pain, and sometimes I feel it's not worth the emotional effort. But how do I go about escaping from reality? Will it take energy? If it does, I'll have to stay sane.

FEBRUARY 12 – *Wednesday*

I dreamt about you last night. This is the first dream I have had since November 22. Since your death I have completely stopped dreaming. Why, I wonder, when I was wont to dream almost every night?

Last night I dreamed you were being buried, and I had forgotten to turn up for the funeral. I was so ashamed of myself and so worried my forgetfulness would be interpreted as uncaring. I wanted to tell everyone that I had forgotten because I'm so tired and strung out. But I didn't have the energy to explain and decided it was easier to let them think the worst of me.

I tortured myself today by browsing through the cards at the university bookstore. I kept reading the ones "for my husband."

My sensibilities are so red raw that I lie awake worrying about stray cats freezing to death and deer floundering in snow drifts. I cry when I hear about the dead and dying in places as distant as El Salvador, and my heart aches for the homeless, the unloved and the lonely. Why should I, a wounded person, want to absorb the pain of the world?

FEBRUARY 15 – *Saturday*

Dreamed about you again last night. This time you weren't dead, but I was losing you in a crowd. You went through a turnstile, thinking I was right behind you. Only I couldn't get the turnstile to work, and I watched, helpless, as you disappeared into the crowd and left me alone in some strange town. I didn't even know where you had parked the car.

FEBRUARY 27 – *Thursday*

My lack of will is really becoming a problem. The school term is moving on, and I'm concerned it will come and go and I won't have any grades to turn in. It's a nightmare situation. I know the work has to be done, but I can't seem to drum up the motivation to get at it. My department head is so very kind and encouraging. He assures me my work will get done on time, and if it doesn't, we'll find a way around it. He has more faith in my resilience than I have.

My ulcers have flared up. I walk the floor at night drinking warm milk and eating crackers, and I wonder as I wander. Who will take care of me if I get sick? Will I end up in a downtown rooming house? Logic tells me I have enough financial resources to prevent this, but logic and I are not very compatible these days. I'm operating strictly on emotions.

And speaking of finances, I can't bring myself to cash your pension checks. It would be like accepting blood money. Someday soon I'm going to have to get this squeamishness behind me, and I know I'm fortunate that I can put it off for a few more months. Some widows don't have this option.

MARCH 1 – *Saturday*

March came in like a lamb, and I'm taking that as a good omen. I have turned over a new leaf. This morning when the alarm went off, I took myself by the scruff of the neck and heaved my unwilling carcass out onto the cold

51

floor. (There's five pounds more to heave these days. All that comfort food has taken its toll.) Once I was up, I reset the alarm and gave myself an hour to get ready for work. "Enough of this," I scolded. "It's high time you took hold."

At the office I made a list of things I was going to make myself do before the day ended. I didn't get the list completed, but I did get enough done to give me some satisfaction. What surprised me was that I could absorb what I read. Since November I have had to read things over and over in order to get comprehension. The words would only hit the surface of my brain and then ricochet back at me, a mixture of unintelligible syllables.

MARCH 3 – *Monday*

Someone called last night about buying the house. My heart dropped to my toes. Sell my home! Our home! This morning when I left for work, I walked backwards along the sidewalk, glutting myself on the sight of the house half-hidden behind the maple and birch trees that are still bare. Those trees must be seventy feet tall now. I so clearly remember when we planted them. How can I sell this house when so much of us is entangled within every board and sod? I lost so much of my identity when you left that I'm afraid the last of me will disappear if I sell this house. If I do disappear with the house, I know I won't have the strength to raise myself from my own ashes.

Someone who is a stranger to sorrow told me today that losing a child is worse than losing a spouse. It's a fact. She said she read it somewhere. I said I supposed it depended on the quality of relationships, and speaking from my own experience, I could not imagine the death of a child altering to any great extent a woman's financial, physical or social environment. I added that, because I haven't lost a child, I couldn't offer comparisons on emotional pain.

However, I really do think that losing a spouse leaves you more bereft, but who is to say for sure. You lose not only your companion, your lover, the father of your children, the person who connects you to a clutch of in-laws, but yourself as well. On top of your grief, you have to cope with finding a new identity.

MARCH 4

Almost spring. A lovely soft day.

The snow on the roads has melted into rivulets of muddy water. My navy blue reefer coat was polka-dotted with mud after the walk to work. The cars hissed the water in all directions as they passed me.

Those who have been there tell me that the changing seasons are positively the worst of times – worse even than the firsts: first anniversary, first birthday, etc. I recall words from Shelley: *Winter is come and gone, But grief returns with the revolving year.*

When I opened the porch door this morning, I felt the softness in the air, and then sadness engulfed me. I was sad for you because you will not be around to see the sun hit our lawn and shrink that mound of dirt-encrusted snow, and I was sad for me because I will have to watch it disappear alone.

MARCH 5 — *Wednesday*

I decided on the spur of the moment today to take Ben and Susan to Arizona. You had promised to have them visit us at this time, so I will keep the promise for you. I'm going full speed ahead with the trip plans, even though I'm not totally convinced I can face the Southwest without you.

With the trip in mind, I tried to balance my cheque book. What an unsightly mess! I am spending money like it's going out of style. One part of me worries about soup kitchens and mission shelters and the other part spends money as if King Tut were my father.

The raw fact is that your death reduced my financial potential by about two-thirds. Still I shop and shop and shop. Sadly enough, the shopping brings no pleasure. I'm told that endless shopping is a phase in early widowhood.

It's a way to try and fill the emotional hunger. I pray, and my bank account prays, that it's a short phase.

I've decided that one reason I'm always so tired is because I'm always on the go. If I have nothing else to do, I'll walk until I'm exhausted. I recall a widow from my childhood. She was on the go so much that the villagers called her Gravel Annie. Will I be called Pavement Jean?

I realized today that your death has not only robbed me of my present and my future, but of my past as well. Who else remembers my parents, remembers my children as babies?

Although my housemate and I are very congenial, I still hate sharing my home. People think it is easy for me to share this house. But I feel I've lost not only a husband, I've lost a home as well. I feel so destitute. Of course, I keep these thoughts deep inside me and allow them to surface only in the still of the night, when my pillow can muffle their sound.

MARCH 7 – *Friday*

Went to a small gathering tonight at the university. I talked. I smiled. Once or twice I even laughed. I felt like a Halloween pumpkin – hollowed out on the inside but looking quite bright and cheery from the outside.

I met a colleague whose wife – a beautiful young woman – died several years ago. He confessed he began dating three weeks after her death.

"That was obscene," I accused, not understanding.

He answered in a soft voice. "I know," he said, and there were traces of guilt in his voice. "But I wanted to deaden the pain." He added, "It didn't help at all."

We leave for Arizona in the morning. I am filled with a thousand insecurities. I have travelled so little without you. Will I be able to navigate the several airport terminals between here and there? Will I be able to smile when I'm greeted by the same friends who were always on hand to greet the two of us?

MARCH 16 – *Sunday*

Arizona was a mistake. Too soon. You walked beside me every inch of the way. At times I hurt so much I was certain my frame would be rent apart.

To top everything, I got the flu soon after my arrival, and I had to let the children come home alone. This year, I seem to be getting every flu and germ that passes within a thousand feet of me.

MARCH 17 – *Monday*

I am so sad tonight. I'm sadder tonight that I've been for the last four and a half months. Friends called to ask me to the St. Patrick's dance. Last year the warm-up party was at our house. What a difference a year makes!

I have such confusing thoughts right now. In the midst of this intolerable grief, I want to be caught up again in good times. On the one hand I want to hold on to my sorrow because holding on to it means holding on to you. On the other hand, I'm wishing it were five years down the road so this pain would be behind me. At least I'm hoping it will be. But such hoping makes me feel guilty. Does this confusion mean I'm healing? At least I'm now aware there is life out there, even if I still don't have the wherewithal to go in search of it.

MARCH 18 – *Tuesday*

I read somewhere that people who are emotionally strong have a difficult time with grief. The article stated that the emotionally strong have always been able to take control over things. But emotional pain doesn't easily lend itself to being controlled, so such people can't use the same rational thinking they would use to solve a physical problem. Also, it said, strong people won't permit themselves to give in to grief, and therefore it takes them longer to come to accept its presence. I think I had better be prepared for a long siege.

In the beginning, the pain was so fierce it obliterated

every other sensation. Now that fierceness is waning, and I am filled with a more low-grade pain. It is, however, an all-permeating pain, and right now I am certain this will keep me company for the rest of my life. Tomorrow and tomorrow and tomorrow.

I went apartment hunting with A. tonight. I returned a basket case. How can I live in this big house all alone? But how can I settle for life in a filing cabinet? I am so angry with you right now. You took with you the past — the days when the children were young and finances were scarce, but life stretched before us long and glorious. You took with you the present, days full and lush and satisfying.

As for the future, I dread to think it exists.

Good Friday

I am alone.

The children had things to do this weekend and lives of their own to live. I am filled with remorse over the many times we should have gone to your mother's but didn't because we had other things to do, better things than listening to an old woman reminisce about her past because it was more substantial than her future. I beg her forgiveness, wherever she may be.

Easter Saturday

Had lunch with an acquaintance this afternoon. She asked whether my writing is now freer because your presence is gone. It told me more about her marriage than she intended. Marriage to you never stifled my creative, academic or intellectual growth. She and I talked about houses – to sell or not to sell. She said if she were in my situation she would buy a condo and redecorate it to make it an expression of herself. Good advice, I think. Perhaps a new physical world will give me the centre I've been seeking ever since you skated the breath out of yourself.

Easter Sunday

I went to church by myself. Afterwards, I visited your grave and placed a rose on it. When I returned home, a friend phoned and asked me to her house for lunch. I also found an Easter egg hanging on my gate. It seems that just at the very time I am certain I cannot bear another moment of life, another moment of being alone, someone rescues me from myself.

I dreamed about you last night. A strange dream. You went to Halifax, and I received word that you had died there. I felt again all the horror and upheaval of those November days. In the midst of my pain, you returned. You had only been in hospital. Instead of feeling joyous at your return, I felt anger because now I understood how terrible it would be to lose you. Nothing would ever be the same in my world again. I could never again know the peace of taking you for granted. When I woke up, my ulcer was in the full throes of an acid overdose, the way it always acts when I experience a rush of anger.

A colleague — a man in the midst of marital separation — asked me to go to the symphony with him tonight. Just for company. I refused because I didn't want anyone to think I was dating so soon after your death. I said if I lived in a larger city I would accept. Afterwards I thought about that statement. A month ago I wouldn't have left this house to attend a symphony even if I were living in Paris. Sometimes I wish I were a grass widow rather than a sod one. I wouldn't feel any responsibility to your memory. And knowing you left me willingly would in some twisted way be a comfort.

Actually, it's not so much about what people think of me as what will people think of you if your widow lacks proper decorum in matters pertaining to your memory. I don't want them to say, "He couldn't have been a very good husband if . . ." This thinking is even filtering down to the way I dress. I ask myself before going out, "Is this suitable for a recent widow? Is it too fashionable? Too colourful? Too solemn?"

Too fashionable? Too colourful? Too solemn? I wish I could move forward to a time when I'll once again wear whatever suits my mood at the moment.

It's almost midnight. I just finished vacuuming a house that didn't need vacuuming. I am so very lonely. My housemate has gone for the holidays. When I was cleaning Steven's room, I opened his closet to vacuum inside and I saw your clothes still hanging on the rack. I took out your navy blue jacket and draped it around my shoulders as I pushed the vacuum over the rug. If anyone had seen this nightgowned woman draped in a man's jacket, pushing a vacuum with one hand and wiping tears away with the other, they would have carted her off to the funny farm. Did I ever think, even in my wildest imaginings, that clutching an empty jacket would get me through a holiday weekend?

MARCH 25 – *Tuesday*

My friend B. in Ottawa telephoned. She has a good deal on two tickets to Barbados and wants me to go with her. I let her talk me into it, although I feel not the slightest tingle of joy at the prospect. Lord Almighty, how I hate this feeling of nothingness.

B. thought the trip would clear my mind about selling or not selling the house. What anguish! The children don't want me to sell, but then they aren't here when the snow piles on the garage roof and I'm worrying whether the rafters will cave in, and they aren't here when the dark settles in. And they aren't here when the empty rooms echo with memories.

APRIL 1 – *Tuesday*

Returned from Barbados. You can't outrun grief. You can't shoo it aside like a pesky fly. I have to try and face it down.

I now understand what Keats meant when he wrote, *To sorrow I bade good-morrow, And thought to leave her far away behind. But cheerly, cheerly, She loves me dearly; She is so constant to me, and so kind.*

Loneliness is two women at a beautiful resort. We went to the opening party put on by the tour people. The first number the band played was "Yellow Bird."

Memories. Memories. Memories.

I talked to a woman in circumstances similar to mine. She's a painter, and she solved the vacation problem by going to areas where artists gather – workshops and the like. I'm thinking of doing likewise for writing.

While I was in Barbados, I lay in bed each night and, at a cost of $250 per day, wished the time away. It was too soon for me to vacation. And it was terribly unfair to B. Sometimes I caught myself being angry at her because she wasn't you, and I would castigate myself for being so unreasonable.

APRIL 3 – *Thursday Morning*

A new day is dawning, and you heard it here first. Full speed ahead and damn the torpedoes. No more sad songs. No more laments. This house deserves better than an echo of happiness past. Let the dead bury the dead. But how am I going to bring this about? How indeed?

APRIL 3 – *Thursday Night*

Well, I made a start already. Today I sent in my application to attend the Learned Societies Conference in Winnipeg, and I've volunteered to chair a session. Certainly I'm terrified of going alone, and I wish I could continue to crouch within the shelter of your wing. But I have to accept the fact that life will never again go back to normal, or at least to my perception of normal. For today at least, normal is pain, and I have to learn to accept that.

APRIL 4 – *Friday*

This morning I removed the family picture from the dining room wall. I could not stand one more day of all those smiling people peeking around the kitchen door watching me eat my solitary breakfast. That picture – the five of us together in the fall – the most beautiful season of the year – is the saddest and most treasured possession I have. And it makes no difference that I know the smile had to be bribed from Ben, threatened from Susan and shamed from Steven, all of them with more important things to do than to go to an abandoned farm and smile for a photographer. Perhaps one day I'll be able to look at it without crying. When that day comes, I'll rehang the picture.

APRIL 5 – *Saturday*

Packed a little more of my old life away today. Another picture – the one of you and me and Steven on Steven's graduation day. I remember that day so well. You and I sat side by side in the faculty row, and our hands touched with pride when our son walked across the stage, a full-fledged civil engineer. Like father like son.

Some people will not understand why I have to remove these pictures. "Too soon to forget," they'll say. Will I be able to reply, "No. Too soon to remember"?

APRIL 7 – *Monday*

For lo the winter has passed. The rains have come and gone. But where is the voice of that damn turtle? The day is so beautiful, I'm certain I'll hear a croak before night falls.

Today I can even believe that after spring there'll be a summer. Winter was fiercely cold. It matched my heart. A warm summer is predicted. How I wish I could be in harmony with the upcoming season.

I made out a new will. Ever since my internal world went into a state of flux, I have had a pressing need to bring order to my external surroundings.

This afternoon I made lists of important papers and financial holdings in the hope the children won't have to search desk drawers should morning come without me around to help usher it in. I emptied my safety deposit box and removed the obsolete material. I even cleaned out all the closets and drawers in the house. I threw out (or gave away) the clothes I know now I'll never shorten, lengthen, let out or take in; the pictures I'll never frame; the crocheted squares (your mother's) that I'll never turn into an afghan, and the photographs I'll never paste in an album. It was like facing up to a lie. Deep down I think I always knew I'd never do these things, but as long as I had a future, I could fool myself into believing I would get to them someday. When the weather gets warmer, I'll attack the garage and throw into a heap the half-finished projects you were certain you would do in some vague and distant future.

It is possible that this purge is a red herring to keep me from facing the decision on the house? Sell? Keep? Take a roomer? Buy a smaller home? Rent an apartment? None of the above?

Night after night I lie in bed going over the same unpalatable options. I face the morning tired and angry. How can I be expected to know what I should or should not do? I'm a grieving person. A walking wound. Just because the distracted and disconnected look has gone from my face doesn't mean I'm in any fit state to make important decisions.

APRIL 15 – *Tuesday*

I know two recent widows – one grass and one sod. Both of them count day endings. "Another day in," they sigh gratefully, if somewhat soulfully. "Another day in for what?" I want to ask. One day's ending is another day's beginning. If I were waiting for a short term something-or-other, I could count down the days, but not when I'm dealing with a distant and undefinable future.

APRIL 19 – *Saturday*

Another dream. I woke up this morning and looked at the clock. It was 8:10. I mumbled, "Oh God! It's Saturday again." Depressed, I willed myself back to sleep. I dreamed that I dreamed you were dead, and when I awoke from my dream I was so delighted I had only been dreaming that I wrapped my arms around you and

66

mumbled, "I had the most terrible dream." But it wasn't you. A stranger was in my bed. The scene changed immediately, and you and I and Ben were climbing the outside of a church steeple. Ben sprinted ahead, and just as I screamed, "Be careful!" he tumbled from the scaffolding and landed in a pond below. Again the scene changed, and I'm down by the pond watching the still body of Ben – clad only in red bathing trunks – floating face up in the water. I reach down and scoop him up in my arms and sit on the shore and begin crooning, "Come back Paddy Riley to Ballyjamesduff. Come back Paddy Riley to me." My mother used to sing that song as she went about the house cleaning and dusting.

APRIL 20 – *Sunday*

A seasoned widow phoned today. She said she had read two books, looked at three television movies, washed her hair, made buttermilk biscuits, and when she looked at the time it was only four p.m. She wondered how she was going to put in the evening. Thank God for my work, my friends and my writing. And speaking of work, I managed to get the assignments corrected, the tests marked and the grades in on time. Now if I only could shake this tiredness, or whatever it is that is sapping my energy. One minute I'm convinced a hot bath is what is needed to rejuvenate me, the next it is a piece of pie, and when that

isn't the answer I'm certain a walk is exactly what I need —
if only I had the energy to go for one.

APRIL 23 — *Wednesday*

When I came out of the bank today, I saw you walking up
the street, leaning into the wind. My foolish heart leapt
until I chastized it for being so silly.

I still search crowds for you, and from time to time, I
catch fleeting glances of the back of your head, the set
of your shoulders, the crook of your smile.

APRIL 26 — *Saturday*

I saw a crocus peeping out of the ground today.

My first instinct was to go back in the house and get
you to come out and see it, just so I could prove to you
they really do grow best beside the chimney. The ones you
planted by the back porch are still dormant.

MAY 1 — *Thursday*

But the merriest month in all the year. . . . Met an acquaintance
downtown today. It was my first encounter with her since
your death. She offered her condolences and went on to

say that she always considered us a study in opposites – big-small, dark-fair – then added that dreaded cliché: life goes on.

I wanted to shout at her, Maybe it does for you. But not for me. Instead I replied, "So they tell me." She continued on her way, glad she wasn't me.

MAY 3 – *Saturday*

Steve came home, and we went to pick out your monument. No small task, as it turned out. I was always under the impression that a monument is a monument is a monument. But *au contraire*.

There are Rolls Royce monuments and Volkswagen monuments and various and sundry models in between. We were given a price list that filled two pages and a catalogue of glossy pictures from which to make our selection. Size: big, medium or small. Double or single. Style: satin-faced or high sheen with polished or unpolished sides. Lettering: large or small. Steven said double size and double names – yours and mine. And both put on now!

I said, "Whoa, there! My name isn't going on any marble slab while I'm above the ground." He acquiesced very reluctantly, stating that he had scouted the cemetery and other wives had their names engraved in waiting. He didn't come right out and say so, but I knew he felt his father deserved no less loyalty from his wife than for her to make a prior commitment to sharing his marble slab. We quickly moved on to the next decision, the motif or design that could be placed at the top of the stone – and this would be thrown in for free.

"The mister," the stone mason said, his voice suitably subdued. "Did he like fishing? I'm good at carving fishing rods." Steven jumped in eagerly. "Hockey?" He fairly shouted the word. "Can you carve a hockey stick or a pair of skates?" "Whoa again," said I. "It was hockey that put your father in the ground, and I have no intention of making a monument to its victory." Although again he grumbled his disagreement, we finally settled for the joined hands motif and your name only, with a space waiting for mine.

MAY 5 – *Monday*

My concentration is fluctuating around the zero mark. I thought by now I would be back to normal.

Certainly the rest of the world expects me to be. But I'm definitely not. I walked across Regent Street this evening without as much as a backward glance at the five o'clock traffic. I actually forgot to look. Someone up there must be protecting me. Yesterday I put on my make-up and then came downstairs and made a cup of coffee.

Ten minutes later, I was back in the bathroom washing my face, completely forgetting I had just done that job.

Someone asked me today, "What stage are you at?" She said this as though I woke up one morning and knew beyond a reasonable doubt that my emotions had left sorrow behind and had now moved into guilt or anger or whatever. Actually, some days I feel anger, sorrow, guilt, acceptance all within the course of a few moments. Other days I'm strong into self-pity. How I feel depends on what has gone on in my day. Sometimes I feel I haven't made any progress since November, and I'm convinced I'll never even find the tunnel, much less the light at the end of it.

MAY 8 – *Thursday*

Spring has temporarily turned into summer. I ran away today. This is the first time I actually, physically ran away since New Year's Eve. The sun was shining through the open windows of my office, and in the halls I could hear people commenting on the glorious weather and saying that things were really shaping up for a beautiful weekend. I don't want a beautiful weekend. A beautiful weekend for what? To be alone? I hurriedly stuffed my briefcase with unfinished work and ran for home as thought the furies were chasing me.

I decided to sit on the back patio, but when I opened the storage doors to get a lawn chair and saw how you had packed away last summer's furniture in anticipation of this summer, I closed the door quickly.

After a spurt of crying, I got into my jogging suit and spent the afternoon walking out my sadness.

People keep telling me I'm strong. I'm so sick of hearing, "But Jean, you're strong." They say this as though hard knocks don't give me pain. I want to shout at them, "I'm not strong. I'm weak. I'm fragile. I'm a pathetic creature. I hurt all over." Maybe I should rent a billboard and have it say, "Jean is not strong. She is a hundred-and-ten-pound weakling." Actually, if I don't soon give up the comfort food, I may still be a weakling, but I certainly won't be a hundred-and-ten-pounds.

MAY 12 – *Monday*

I'm dreaming regularly now – benign dreams. November 22 never happened. For the most part, the subject of the dreams is us when the children were small. Do these dreams mean my unconscious is still refusing to accept your death? Do they mean my mind has come out of its stupor and shock? Do they mean anything at all?

It is so difficult to have to spend day after day on the campus. I see you in all the old familiar places. Mostly I see you heading for the faculty club. I see you rushing (always rushing, your coat open, even in winter, and tie blowing over your shoulder) to join me for lunch.

I think I made significant progress this week. I finally was able to enter the faculty club. I have tried to do this on several occasions but always faltered at the bottom of the steps. My friend S. accompanied me and helped with the re-entry.

MAY 15 – *Thursday*

More progress! I returned to driving today after a ten-year lapse. You always said I would rue the day I sat back and left the driving to you, but it had seemed so much easier to scrape the ice from one car instead of two, especially when we were both going the same route. After a while I lost my nerve.

My friend A. came with me on my maiden voyage. We went around and around the block. I felt positively exhilarated when I returned to the house. Nerve-racked, but exhilarated.

And still more progress! I can now wait until dark before rechecking the locks and doors and windows, and I don't have to put the upstairs hall light on until after dark.

But if I go ahead two steps, I go back one. My body aches for your physical presence. How I wish I could climb into bed and find your waiting arms.

MAY 16 — *Friday*

Got the contract for my book today. I wish I felt like celebrating.

I fixed a strap on a purse this evening. Not much of an accomplishment, I suppose. But I finally realized you weren't going to return to fix it, and it wouldn't grow shorter of its own accord. I got out my tool kit — a fork, a butcher knife, a pair of scissors and your pliers that I found on the patio a couple of days ago, rust-covered from their hiatus in the snow.

People ask whether I find joy in these little accomplishments. I do feel some sense of gaining control, but I'd feel a lot more joy if I could turn the job over to you.

MAY 17 — *Saturday*

My housemate moved out this morning. She would have liked to stay longer, and I would have liked to have her stay, but I steeled myself and kept to our original agreement. Actually, we both knew we had to be on our own — each for different reasons. I could hear the still-ness in the house after she left. I sat on the stairs and allowed myself to cry for a little while, then I took a bath and went for a long walk.

Now I know why it is called a long weekend. It was in-terminable. Last night, alone in the house, I think I reached what the poets call the dark night of the soul. My loss seemed deeper, my future bleaker and my present almost intolerable. I asked myself over and over, "How do I keep going forward? How do I keep walking onwards with the pain of this festering wound?"

I was furious with you all over again. Why did you have to play hockey when I was so adamant that you were too old for such strenuous exercise?

And I was furious with your teammates who had encouraged you to keep playing. I hated them for saying I was henpecking you when I tried to talk you into quitting. I wanted to go to their homes and haul them out of their secure beds and shout at them, "Look at what you've done to me! Look at what you've done to him!"

And, my God! How I envied their wives. They were home curled up safely beside their husbands. They weren't wandering through an empty house clinging to sanity.

MAY 21 — *Wednesday*

I hosted a small luncheon today. The weekend was so terrible — so filled with despair and hate — that I knew I had to take drastic action to try and turn my life around.

On Tuesday I called a few friends for a patio luncheon. Once I made that first call I couldn't back out, even though I wanted to do just that. It was a lovely afternoon. I only had four guests – all women whose marriages are broken.

Maybe next time I'll stretch my guest list to include women whose lives are intact. Presently, it hurts too much to be around them.

After I cleaned up the luncheon dishes, and while I was on an energy roll, I telephoned a diet centre and signed up for a program of sensible eating. I'm practically living on dairy products. My non-dairy meals usually consist of something from the fast food section of the grocery store: boil a bag, remove and heat, whip and chill or thaw and serve. Perhaps my irritability and my tiredness will go away if I can get back to sensible eating.

Graduation

A very sad day. It is six months to the day since your death. I couldn't walk in the academic procession, but I did torture myself by getting out our doctoral hoods and pressing them. For what reason, pray tell? Am I into self-flagellation or what?

I was asked by a group of married friends to go with them to the alumni dance. I refused. It would be layering pain upon pain. Besides, I didn't want to go to a dance and wait upon the generosity of other wives and upon the accommodation of other husbands. I'd get more pleasure out of going to aerobics classes, and you know how I hate structured exercise classes.

My extreme sadness has put me in a mellow mood. I want to thank you for who I am. Without you, I never would have gone to university, written a novel or learned to play cribbage. I also want to thank you for fostering my self-confidence. And I forgive you for dying – at least I do at this moment. Tomorrow I may be back to, How could you do such a dastardly deed to me?

Before the night is over I might even drum up enough magnanimity to thank God for loaning you to me. It was such a quality loan. But I know my mellow mood won't extend to forgiving myself for not insisting that we take time to sit on the porch on lazy weekends instead of repairing or renovating the house. And for not using the percale sheets instead of keeping them for company. And for not telling you more often and more fervently how much I loved you. Like Richard II, I want to call back yesterday and bid time return.

MAY 24 – *Saturday*

I leave for the Learned Societies Conference in Winnipeg tomorrow. My trembling self is pretending to be one real cool lady.

MAY 31 — *Sunday*

The trip to the Learneds was an even worse mistake than the trip to Barbados or to Arizona. I came down with strep throat and then had an allergic reaction to the antibiotics I was given to clear it up. I ended up in the emergency room of the hospital — via ambulance. Earlier I wrote that I forgave you for dying. In the ambulance I forgave you for dying so suddenly. I was so ill. I could not wish even five minutes of that agony on you — even to permit me a final farewell. At the emergency centre, I was asked for my next of kin. What a jolt that was! "Your next of kin," they kept insisting while I just stared at them mutely. "We must have your next of kin." How could I tell them my next of kin is dead?

How do you tell a group of white-coated humans who are assaulting your body with needles and tubes that your next of kin is dead?

Still, sick or not, I did make it to Winnipeg alone.

JUNE 2 — *Monday*

To all intents and purposes, I'm getting on with my life. I have settled your estate, learned to drive, conditioned myself to staying alone in the house — at least for the time being. I have even highlighted my hair. All outward signs point to my being back to normal — whatever that might

78

mean. The truth is though – the frightening truth is – I think I'm coming unravelled. The struggle to give my life the appearance of normalcy has taken its toll. I'm beginning to hate to go to sleep because I dream about you.

But perhaps it isn't the dreaming I hate; it's the waking. *I slept and dreamt that life was beauty. I woke and found that life was duty*. I'm not certain, but I think Emily Dickinson wrote those words. They've been circling my brain all evening.

I'm starting to have anxiety attacks. And I can't sit still. I'm filled with nervous tension. I can't content myself at the office. I can't content myself at home. Sometimes the restlessness inside me is overwhelming. On Sundays I have to sit in the back of the church so that if need be I can make a quick getaway. If this continues, I don't know how I'm going to cope with my classes in the fall. It's been almost seven months! Why can't I grab hold? Perhaps the house question being unsettled is driving me to this distraction.

I wish I could get interested in my writing – or something. I ask myself over and over, What do I do with the rest of my life? I know with certainty that teaching isn't enough. I dread the thought of an empty life. I can spot a bleak life a block away. One woman confessed she goes to three different church services just to get her through Sunday. From goblins and ghosties and three legged beasties and from church hopping on Sundays, dear God protect me. Apologies, Robbie Burns.

I visited your grave today and brought you a rose. From time to time I drop by to see you just so you won't have to make excuses to your neighbours about lack of visits from your family. In my black moments, I'm certain that's how I'll end up: in a nursing home, making excuses for the relatives who never come to see me.

JUNE 22 – *Sunday*

Seven months today since you died. Remember the colleague I told you about who began dating three weeks after his wife's death? I was talking to him today, and he was telling me that a few weeks after his wife died he asked a friend – a widower of six months – how long it took to get over the pain. The friend had no answer, just walked away. Months later my colleague asked him why he had acted so. Replied the friend, "How could I tell you I didn't know? At that time all I knew was it took longer than six months, and you didn't want to hear that."

I really think I'm coming unglued, and the frightening thing is that on the outside I still look as if I'm "taking it well." I was asked to a cottage for the weekend, but my nerves are so red raw I can't commit myself to being a house guest. I need the privacy to pace. Perhaps I should go to a doctor for a pill of some sort, but I believe I have to help myself out of this black pit. The weather the last few days has been fine, and last evening I went out to police the lawns and fix up the ravages of winter. I listlessly picked up a fallen branch here and there. After a few minutes I gave up all pretence of caring whether the lawn looked unkempt or not. I came in the house and drew a bath, hoping that the warm water would help keep the parts of me together.

JUNE 23 – *Monday*

More vultures circling.

I had a call from a person who had heard I was going to sell the house and move into an apartment. He wanted to have first crack at buying my excess furniture. I told him it was a vicious rumour that I was selling any of my belongings – house or furniture. In truth, I would make a bonfire of the furniture before I would sell it garage-sale style. I couldn't bear to have strangers haggle over our precious memories. If push comes to shove, I'll give the stuff up for adoption to family and friends.

After that phone call, I went to the store and bought a double-decker box of Laura Secord French Mints and ate the whole thing. If I don't get such unbridled decadence under control, I'll need a new wardrobe, and I don't have any spare energy to devote to shopping.

JUNE 24 – *Tuesday*

My father's birthday. He was fifty-two when he died. I wish I had understood my mother's pain then. Tennyson said, *'Tis held that sorrow makes us wise*. The only trouble is that wisdom comes too late and at too great a price.

JUNE 27 – *Friday Morning*

I've decided that what I need is a full day of crying. It will relieve me of the jitters. I'm setting aside tomorrow. I'm going to lock the doors, turn off the phone, close the drapes and let the tears flow. I'll weep myself dry. Maybe then my eyes won't fill up and my voice crack when someone asks how I'm doing without you.

JUNE 27 – *Evening*

Just had a call from Roge and family. They are arriving from Montreal tomorrow to spend Canada Day weekend with me. I guess that scuttles my plans for the crying binge.

JUNE 28 – *Saturday*

When I woke up this morning, my first thought was, Roge and family are coming this afternoon. My second thought was that you had died, and the third was wondering how I would get through their visit without your presence. Who, for instance, would do the barbecuing? Still, you *were* my second thought. In January I said that before spring arrived I'd wake up to a thought other than your death. So I missed my deadline by a season, but who's counting?

JULY 4 – *Friday*

Steve saved the day yesterday by coming home unexpectedly. He did the barbecuing. When we sat down to eat, everyone talked louder and faster than usual. We rapidly filled in all the silent spaces, fiercely pretending we didn't notice the empty saddle.

JULY 5 – *Saturday*

It is thundering and lightning and there's a savage wind. And the house is so silent. So empty. The branches from the lilac tree are scraping against the window panes and making intruder noises. What if the lights go out?

I think the candle stubs went out in the cleaning purge. I need you tonight. I really need you. I need to be hugged. I need to be loved. I need to feel safe.

I'm so terribly afraid of the night, especially of the night in this house. The boogeyman skulks in the basement waiting for the lights to go out. But I fool him. I keep all lights burning. The place looks like the *Titanic* just before it hit the iceberg. Yesterday I stocked up on fuses, and as soon as I returned from the store, I decided to try my hand at fuse replacement before the need actually arose. But I couldn't find the fuse box. I called our neighbour and asked him if he knew where it was.

He was silent for several seconds, and when he finally spoke, he sounded as though he were talking to a small child who had lost her way. "Jean, my dear," he said, "when you had the new furnace put in last year, you also replaced the fuse box with a circuit breaker. You no longer need fuses. You just flick a switch."

Slightly nonplussed, I replied, "In that case, do you know of anyone who can use two dozen fuses of varying amps?"

JULY 10 – *Thursday*

Went to the bank today and had my credit cards reinstated. When you died I had an overpowering urge to simplify my life. When I cancelled your credit cards, I cancelled my own as well. I even cancelled the newspaper because I couldn't cope with the burden of having to remember to pay the carrier.

But my penchant for simplicity still hasn't totally deserted me. Today I made one final culling of drawers and closets. With the zeal of an evangelist ridding a village of devils, I cast out threadbare towels, mismatched dishes, leaky vases and pots with burnt bottoms. Without a backward glance I threw out lamps without sockets, empty jam jars, dozens of plastic ice cream containers.

I didn't even have a tear in my eye when I dumped the placemats with the wobbly-stitched hems Susan had given me for Christmas – a grade one project. With equal callousness I dumped the plaster cast of Steven's hand, his kindergarten birthday present for me.

JULY 11 – *Friday*

Earlier tonight an acquaintance dropped in because she happened to be in the neighbourhood. I think she dropped in because she wanted to inquire about the house. In the course of conversation, she said I should really try to get on with my life because "sooner or later it happens to all of us." It was on the tip of my tongue to say, "I would have preferred if it had happened to you sooner and me later," but my tongue isn't that sharp yet. In the next breath, she said she had to go home because her husband was there alone watching television. What were you doing about that time?

JULY 15 – *Tuesday*

Your brother and family visited today. Frank did the barbecuing, and when I saw him doing what you should be doing, I got a pain in my heart so piercing I could barely breathe. He looks so much like you, but he isn't you.

JULY 16 – *Wednesday*

A black letter day! I put the house on the market this afternoon. When I woke up this morning I knew beyond a shadow of a doubt that I had to sell. My friend A. said the day would come when I would have an answer to the house question. She also added there would be no joy in the answer. How prophetic she was.

Yesterday should have been a very happy day. Relatives were here. Steve dropped in unexpectedly. A group of Steven's friends came by. But all the company did for me was to make me aware that this house will never be my house. It was our house, and the joy it gave us will never be transferred to me alone.

JULY 17 – *Thursday*

Your funeral has been on my mind all evening. I recall how I was convinced you were just visiting the funeral parlour, and at any minute you would return to the house and join the party at our place. I think the Valium I had been encouraged to swallow helped detach me from reality, or maybe it was my unwillingness to face reality that made me resort to the Valium. Will I be able to cope with the actuality of losing this house? Will I have to resort to Valium? Alcohol? All of the above?

JULY 20 – *Sunday*

No buyer for the house as yet, but I have convinced myself that I will be well rid of it.

My friend A. left this morning for Toronto. She is relocating there. She stayed with me overnight, and when she drove out of the driveway I couldn't watch her departure. I came in the house, and an Irish jig was playing on the radio. Guess what I did?

I step-danced. Yes! Step-danced! Tears streamed down my face. What a madwoman!

Later, in the afternoon, I painted the lampposts in the driveway and the veranda railing. I even replaced a broken back step. I'm so tired tonight I may even sleep.

AUGUST 1 – *Friday*

M.J. – niece and godchild – came to visit. The two of us took off for Maine. It was a sentimental journey because we visited all of the places you and I frequented. Went to our favourite restaurant and were seated at a table for three! I could almost reach over and touch your hand. But all in all, it was the most pleasant few days I have had since November 22.

AUGUST 2 – *Saturday*

The first thing I do every morning when I wake up is to determine whether it is a weekday, a weekend or a civic holiday. Civic holidays are positively the worst, closely followed by the weekends.

A nice surprise! A package arrived from Toronto. Giorgio perfume from A. Extravagant woman! I'm having lunch today with another friend – the one who gave me this journal. As I said earlier, how fortunate I am to have friends.

AUGUST 10 – *Sunday*

Have had several prospective buyers for the house. I can't deal with their coming, so I make an exit well in advance of their arrival.

AUGUST 12 – *Tuesday*

Summer is ending. I dread the beginning of the university year. I still fantasize about things being "back to normal." In actual fact, from time to time I find myself thinking, I'll do this or that when things get back to normal. And I still can't find solace anywhere. Everyone should have a place where they can feel safe and secure and at peace. I used to be able to find all of these in this house.

AUGUST 14 – *Thursday*

Finally cleaned out the garage. I even painted the concrete floor. It looks so great, I envy the new owner.

AUGUST 16 – *Saturday*

I went to the market today. It was the first time since November. The new produce was piled high in the different stalls. A couple I knew spoke to me, and because this was the first time I had seen them since your death, they offered their condolences. Later I saw them buying cut flowers, smugly sure of their togetherness — at least it appeared so to me. That hurt! It seems everywhere I turn I run into pain.

Neighbours had a party. They didn't ask me, although last year we both were asked. They reasoned that I wouldn't have wanted to go. I wouldn't have, but I still would have liked to be asked.

AUGUST 27 – *Wednesday*

Lately I've been flirting with death, or, more aptly, death has been flirting with me. Yesterday I drove up along the St. John River. The water had that soft summer-evening calm you see in late August when the wind has died down and dusk is just beginning to drift in. As I drove along, glancing from time to time from the road to the river, I idly wondered whether there was as much quiet and peace at the bottom of the river as there seemed to be at the top. In the midst of my wondering, a seductive, siren-like voice — the voice Circe must have used to lure sailors to their death — whispered in my ear. "No need to keep wondering about the river, Jean. Find out for yourself. Just ease your grip on the steering wheel." Obediently, but ever so gingerly, I loosened my grip.

The soothing voice coaxed, "Loosen up a little more. A tiny bit more." Just as I was uncurling my fingers, a commanding voice ordered, "Don't do it! What if you bungle the job? Think of the consequences!" Afterwards I wondered whether it was your voice that gave the command. It did have that reasoned and reasonable tone of an engineer. But no matter who spoke the words, they were good words. What if I did indeed botch the job? I thought about the two women I know who recently, but for different reasons, tried to abort their stay here, each unsuccessfully, and now their lives are worse than before. I jerked the wheel to the left and made a quick U-turn and headed back home, hugging the far edge of the road all the way.

But the temptress returned again today. I was walking to work, and just before I was to cross the main street of the campus – the one between the bookstore and the forestry building – an indescribable sadness enveloped me. The weight of it shackled me to the spot. I stood there unable to go forwards or backwards, like the Ancient Mariner with that damn albatross on his neck. The paralysis panicked me, and I snapped an order at myself to think of something, *anything*, that could bring a little joy into my life, and it didn't matter how ridiculous or outrageous it might be.

I dredged up decadent and deliciously sinful acts deigned to send the blood coursing through my veins. A half gallon of butter pecan ice cream with a can of extra sauce. My stomach lurched. I've binged once too often this year.

An affair! A short but blazing affair. I tried to come up with names for my little tryst, but none would come to mind. Besides, where would I get the energy to go out and buy new lingerie?

I dropped down on the grass. Nothing or no one could help me. Despair flooded my being. Then a picture blasted into my brain. It was a neon sign, and the word DEATH beckoned tantalizingly in an array of colours. Peace replaced the despair. No more worrying whether I was doing the right thing by selling the house. No more phantom footsteps on the staircase. No more higgledy-piggledy cheque book. No more student assignments. No more searching for umbrellas, gloves, credit cards and other belongings that won't stay close to me. And no more missing you.

I stood up and, without a thought for the traffic, walked out into the street. Cars careened around me. Brakes squealed. Drivers shouted. I walked across that crowded street as unperturbed as a cat strolling across a window ledge.

Later in my office I chastized myself severely. Enough of this nonsense! Enough already! I ordered. There's a season for everything, and life is not yours to arrange or rearrange.

SEPTEMBER 1 – *Monday*

I went for a long walk today on the outskirts of town. It was a golden autumn day, and it brought to mind words from D.H. Lawrence. *Autumn always gets me badly as it breaks into colours.*

Are you aware that by dying in November you spoiled my very special season? I'll never again be able to look at October without thinking that November is not far behind. Until November 22, only good things happened to me in the fall: my first job, meeting you, marrying you, entering university.

Fall is now a season of endings. I wonder whether when university opens, I'll be able to take delight in the smell of new books and the taste of chalk dust. Will I still enjoy meeting new students and reuniting with old ones?

SEPTEMBER 9 – *Tuesday*

Today I made it through the university gates. I've been having more anxiety attacks lately, and when I met with my first class I could feel the shortness of breath beginning.

I prayed as I walked along the corridor to my class-room. Dear God, let me get through this class. Don't let my heart start pounding. Don't let me feel as if the walls are folding around me, choking me to death. Don't let me make a spectacle of myself by pulling a panic attack. I had the bad humour to end with, God you owe me that much!

All during class I had a difficult time concentrating on my subject matter. All I could think about was coming home to an empty house, a house with a silent voice, and not being able to share my day with you, and how pointless and useless everything is. But I made it through the period, so perhaps the next time won't be so difficult. And perhaps God does remember that I was left bereft a few months ago and that He (or She) really does owe me one.

SEPTEMBER 14 – *Sunday*

Just returned from an evening out with very dull people – widows all. Friends refer widows to me now as if I'm a collector of them, as if I no longer want to be discriminating in my friendships. The only thing I had in common with tonight's dinner companions was that death had also snatched their spouses. As the time dragged on, I kept saying to myself, For this I'm missing *Sixty Minutes* and *Murder She Wrote*.

In the beginning, when acquaintances sent widows to me, it didn't matter that the only bond between us was our dead husbands. We talked only about them anyway. But now things are changing. I want to choose my own friends again. Does this mean I'm healing? Or does it only mean I don't want to go around in a gaggle of widows simply because I am one myself?

Shortly after you died, I joined a widows' group. I thought anything was worth a try. But some of the women there had been widowed ten, twelve and fifteen years. I thought, God forbid. I don't want to make a career out of widowhood. I never went back.

SEPTEMBER 15 – *Monday*

Took the car in for its annual rust inspection today and for a heavy waxing to combat the wear and tear of the salty roads to come. This time last year I had never heard of a rust inspection check. See what a fast learner I am?

P.S. It's my birthday.

P.P.S. I need a hug.

SEPTEMBER 16 – *Tuesday*

I walk late at night because I don't want the neighbours to feel sorry for me, but then when I'm out on the lonely streets I start feeling sorry for myself. Sometimes I'm so blinded by tears I stumble off the sidewalk. I often scold myself for my self-indulgence, but then I ask, Why not feel sorry for myself? "You'd feel sorry for a stranger," I say, "if you knew he was hurting, so why not spare some sympathy for the person you love best?"

I envy widows who wish they'd find a new relationship. They have hope. At this point, I only wish for you. How barren and hopeless my life is.

SEPTEMBER 18 – *Thursday*

Depression is settling in for a long siege unless I can find a way to master it. I come home from work, and I just sit and stare. Sometimes I just sit. I have a buyer for the house, and he is pressing for an answer. I won't dicker on the price. Perhaps I'm hoping he'll get tired of waiting. I think that holding onto the house is my way of holding onto the last remnants of you and me.

OCTOBER 1 – *Wednesday*

The anxiety attacks appear to be lessening. I just won't sit still for them any more. If I'm lying in bed and I feel one coming on, I get up and make myself a cup of tea. I still wake up at night and hear your footsteps moving about in the kitchen, going to the bathroom, checking the doors before coming upstairs. I start to drop drowsily back to sleep, knowing all is well with the world because you and the children are safe in the fold. Then I come bolt awake. There is no you downstairs. There are no children in the fold.

I came across an old cheque book of yours that somehow escaped the purge. Seeing your handwriting unnerved me. They say time heals, but no one says how much time is needed for that. I know now that if I hadn't sorted your things early on, I could never bring myself to do so at this time. It seems now that I finally realize you have gone, I want to horde whatever remains of you, even if it's just your handwriting.

OCTOBER 4 – *Saturday*

Our wedding anniversary! I got through the morning by washing sweaters and hanging them out to dry in the golden sunshine. I didn't fare so well in the afternoon, and at one point I found myself going up the stairs whimpering like a wounded animal. A friend of ours phoned. She didn't know it was our anniversary, and I didn't tell her. She informed me she was going to an engineering dance this evening. How that hurt! I remembered how handsome you looked last year at the dance, and you would have looked even better this year in your brand new tuxedo. I couldn't recall having told you that night that I thought you were handsome.

Looking back now, I know I was stingy with my compliments. It's just something else with which to flog myself.

I wallowed all afternoon, I even tortured myself by digging out our wedding photographs. Was your hair ever that black? Was I ever that young? Then the rain came down – a real downpour. It rained the day of our wedding, too. Finally, I could stand neither myself nor the house one instant longer, so I jumped in the car and went to mass. As bad luck would have it, when I entered the church, the soloist – the same man who sang at your funeral – was singing the same hymn, "Like a Shepherd." I turned around and drove home. But I couldn't go back in the house. I screeched the tires and backed out of the driveway and went to a friend's house – one who is working her way through a sorrow. I was crying so hard I couldn't even get out of the car. I just lay on the steering wheel and cried and cried and cried. My friend saw my car and came and got me. She poured me a stiff drink of orange juice and rum and stood over me until I downed the whole glass.

OCTOBER 6 – *Monday*

The foliage is so beautiful this year. The reds are redder and the yellows yellower than I can ever remember them being. It's like looking at an artist's interpretation of fall. I am grateful I can once again see in colour, not just the black and grey that formed my palette in the early weeks after you died. Students milled about the campus all afternoon, chatting outside on the lawn. Some hung out of the dormitory windows and shouted to the passersby, telling about their plans for the weekend. The girls looked lovely in this year's fashion colours: cobalt blue, fuschia pink, pea-pod green. I haven't bought anything new for fall. And I haven't any plans to make for the weekend. I feel alienated from the whole human race.

Thanksgiving

I know I should be thankful for all I had and for all I still have, but the plain truth is I'm an ingrate. Is it so bad to want things to be back to what they once were?

I'm not up to going anywhere for dinner, so I will sit home and eat my boil-and-serve dinner with the six o'clock news for company.

NOVEMBER 3 – *Monday*

I took a shower a few minutes ago, and when I tried to turn off the water, the faucet just kept turning uselessly. Panic! Where would I get a plumber close to midnight?

With much chagrin I remembered the times you had told me where the water shut-off valve is located, and how I had let the information go in one ear and out the other. When would I have need for such knowledge? You would always be on hand to look after things. Ignorance notwithstanding, though, I ran to the basement, and after turning off everything in sight, including the furnace and the electricity, I did luck upon the water valve. It is the last straw! The house goes.

NOVEMBER 7 – *Friday*

The house is sold! Long live an apartment. I have to be out by the last of November. If I sound glib, it's because it's the only way I can survive. I don't want to spend the rest of my life in a filing cabinet *cum* apartment. I want space to breathe. I want a yard.

I'm angry at you all over again. Why couldn't I have been the one to die? I believe you got the best of the deal.

NOVEMBER 8 – *Saturday*

I dreamed about you last night – a strange dream. We were sitting in the living room of a house you had rented for us. It was a shabby house, and I was angry at you for renting it. As we threw sharp words back and forth across the room, I noticed a hatch in the middle of the floor. My instinct was to run out of the house, but you said we had to find out what was beneath the hatch. You kicked the boards in, and to our amazement a startled young woman was looking up at us. She looked like Andrew Wyeth's Helga. She didn't appear to be either frightened or delighted – just startled. I stared back at her, equally startled. I had the feeling the woman was me – an earlier me. The dream still disturbs me, yet I can't put my finger on why it should.

I went to a pot luck supper tonight at E. and I.'s house. I had refused several invitations from them during the past months. E. assured me the social would not be couple-oriented, and she convinced me I needed a break from packing our lives into cardboard boxes. After the initial awkwardness of entering the house, I actually forgot I was carrying around a rooted sorrow. I laughed and talked and drank two glasses of wine. Probably I should say, I drank two glasses of wine, then I laughed and talked and forgot I was carrying around a rooted sorrow. It was difficult returning home alone, but I no longer return to a dark house. Now that I am ready to move, I have learned to leave on the lights when I go out.

NOVEMBER 9 – *Sunday*

Dreamed about you again last night. You were going to lift something heavy, and I screamed at you not to do so because it would hurt your heart. I woke up elated. You were alive. I had prevented you from having a heart attack. I was euphoric. I had hauled you back from the jaws of death. I was given a second chance, and this time I would show you how much you were appreciated. Then reality set in. The low that followed lasted the rest of the night and most of today.

This evening when I was getting my thaw-and-serve supper ready, I heard the squeal of your brakes on the concrete driveway. You had a way of stopping suddenly, as if the garage was always nearer than you thought. I haven't heard your phantom comings and goings for months. Why are they recurring now? Is it on account of selling the house?

Remember that clock radio on your night table? I always said it had no respect for me because it knew I was a technopeasant. Well, today, after about two hours of hit-and-miss setting and resetting of both the time and alarm, and of finally resorting to a thorough reading of the directions, I made it submit to me. I had to find out how to operate it because I'll have to unplug it to move it to my apartment, and then, as per usual, it will go into its blinking act. I feel as buoyant as if I had just exorcised a devil.

NOVEMBER 10 – *Monday*

I'm putting on a dinner party. I don't know where the energy to do this is going to come from, but I want to (actually, I feel driven to) have one more gathering before I let the house go. The dinner will be for those special people who helped me so much during the past year. I have tried for many months to muster the courage to do this. Before November 22 of last year, I could have put on a party dinner almost on the spur of the moment; now it is a major undertaking. I have concerns that have nothing to do with preparation of the food, or even with my chronic tiredness. They have to do with seating: who sits in your place at the head of the table? And with mixing the drinks: who will do your job? And most crucial of all, how will I be able to keep the guests from knowing that my wounds will be wide open and bleeding? In a way, this dinner will be a farewell to the house.

NOVEMBER 16 – *Sunday*

The party went well – surprisingly well. I solved the table problem by having fourteen guests, and each end of the table was shared by two people. Besides, we were all so crowded, I don't think anyone was aware of what I had done to accommodate the empty saddle.

I had a bad moment when I was certain I was going to come unravelled. About a half-hour before the guests arrived, when I had everything in readiness, I went upstairs to get dressed. It was a time when you always shunted me out of the kitchen and announced that you would take over. I got out the dress I was going to wear, but I couldn't manage to pull it over my head. I sat on the edge of the bed and cried desperately lonely tears. Just as panic was settling in around me, the doorbell rang, and there was S. coming to give me a hand. She knows what loss is all about and realized those last moments would be difficult. She made us a pre-party drink, and together we pretended that for me this was any old time and any old party and not a quantum leap into the future.

The guests were a motley group as far as marital status was concerned: a wife whose husband had gone hunting, a husband whose wife was away on university business, a husband and wife, some clergy, single male, single female, etc. Everyone blended and the conversation flowed.

The head of my department served the drinks. Many of the guests offered to help with the clean-up. I refused all offers, but the next time I won't be so apt to turn down such help. It had to be one of the loneliest acts I have ever done – cleaning up by myself at two a.m. No one around to hold post mortems with. No one to say the grasshopper pie was delicious or the molded salad I forgot in the fridge wasn't missed.

NOVEMBER 18 – *Tuesday*

The movers are coming tomorrow. Tonight I put the finishing touches on the packing. I feel battered and buffeted.

At this time, more than any other time in my life, I need the shelter of your wing.

NOVEMBER 20 – *Thursday*

Yesterday I took up residence in my new quarters, a.k.a. the filing cabinet. You know what the apartment building reminds me of? That chicken concentration camp we used to pass en route to your mother's house. Hundreds of little square openings for windows, and all those sad little chicken faces poking out through each opening trying to get a breath of air. You used to laugh at me because, every time that building came in sight, I would threaten to let the chickens loose so they could scratch in the earth and do all the things a hen creature has the right to do before ending up baked or broiled.

The kids, plus Ken, your graduate student, were on hand to help with the moving. After the movers left, the children and I wandered through the rooms on the pretence of a final check for left-behind belongings, but actually we were saying goodbye to our port in a storm for eighteen years and to nooks and crannies filled with memories.

Later that evening, when the children went back to their own lives, I sat in my new living room and surveyed my cramped quarters. It was obvious at first glance that my past life was bigger than my present one. I saw the rug that had to be rolled up on one end to make it fit. I saw the overstuffed chairs lined up side by side as if I were getting ready for a concert. And I saw the mahogany dining room table, pretentious and bulky, squeezed into the area the brochure had called "a dining nook."

When I had everything in order – perhaps I should say in place, because there is no room for order – I made myself a cup of tea.

I was just about to take my first sup when the tenant in the upstairs apartment turned on his stereo. Full blast! Even my jaws began to vibrate. I remembered the day we took my mother to the nursing home. "So this is it!" she said resignedly. "So this is what it has come to!" I swallowed a mouthful of tea, looked at the trembling light fixture in my make-do dining room and mumbled out loud, "So this is it! So this is what it has come to!"

When darkness fell I began to feel sorry for the house. Did it feel abandoned? Was it wondering why we had left? Where we had gone? What it had done to bring about such desertion? Before I realized the stupidity of what I was doing, I was in the car heading back home.

I never turned on the lights because I didn't want the neighbours to get concerned. I sat on the stairs in the dark, and the house and I tried to comfort each other. We recounted the living that had gone on within its walls over the past eighteen years. We recalled the happy times and the sad times. The times of tribulation. The times of jubilation. The times of tears. The times of laughter. The times of anger and the times of peace. It took almost an hour to cover the years, but when we were finished we both were ready to call it a night.

I learned a terrible truth while I was sitting on the stairs. A human being is capable of feeling complete sadness but not complete happiness. Happiness is always tinged with sorrow, with if onlys, with awareness that this moment is transient. But sadness is not generous enough to allow in other emotions. Sadness enfolds you like a shroud.

NOVEMBER 22 – Morning

It is one year ago tonight. But last night – Friday – was the more meaningful date.

Ben stayed with me last night, and after he went to bed I turned on *Dallas*, just as I had done last year, but this time I paid scant attention to what was on the screen. My mind was waiting for the knock on the door that would tell me you had been rushed to the hospital. When ten o'clock came and went and there was no knock, I turned off the television and climbed into bed. I wanted to say something to you in this journal to mark the occasion, but the words wouldn't form. I wished I could have wiped out the past year just as the writers of *Dallas* had done. I wished I could have turned all of the happenings into a dream and changed the ending of the story. I cried long into the night. I cried because I am too young to be a widow and too old to be a lover and too tired to give a damn one way or another

I visited your grave today and left a rose in the snow. Two recent widows who remembered the date took me to a quiet restaurant for supper. Both women had been through the first anniversary, and each agreed that the first year had lessened their horror and deepened their sorrow and that, according to all reports, it takes two years to get on top of the grief. We talked about you. I admitted that I'm shaping you from the perspective of distance and loss and that, like a painter, I'm selecting my landscape with care, choosing to put on paper only what I find appealing. Maybe later I won't be so selective, and I'll grumble about your penchant for having to be early – and I do mean early, not just on time – for all occasions, and I might even recall how you had to be coaxed to take vacations because you found your work to be more enjoyable than traipsing around Europe. I'll probably also remember the disagreements we had on account of your focus on the present, which conflicted so fiercely with my focus on the future. And I'll recall that you weren't good at handling the household accounts. If I really put my mind to it, I may be able to come up with other short-comings that were lesser or greater than those just mentioned. But for the time being, I'll remember you the way that suits me best.

Tonight, because I'm in a reflective mood, I reread the

jottings in this journal. I was reminded of my mother's letters — the ones she used to write from the loneliness of her empty house, her children having left the nest and her husband having taken up residence in that mansion of many rooms. You called her letters, "woeful tales from a Newfoundland village." And I would laugh. Now I feel guilty for us both. She would tell us her days were long but her nights were longer, that her ulcer wouldn't lead nor drive no matter how much baking soda she swallowed, that if the rain didn't soon let up, her vegetable garden would go to stalk, that the wind was so bad the spruce logs left the stove and went up the chimney whole, untouched by flame, and that the sun hadn't shone since the caplin rolled in on the beach in mid-June. But no matter how long she went on in the hens-won't-lay vein, she always felt compelled to end on an upbeat note, and she would write a few last sentences, stowing in the good things that had happened. She had a winning streak at bingo. A neighbour brought her a piece of fresh salmon. Mrs. Bridie's Bride didn't have the cancer after all, it was only a tumour filled with harmless water.

Now, like her, I'm going to stow in a few sentences to let you know that there have been a few streaks of silver in that jet black lining. I want you to know I couldn't have trudged the path without the constancy of friends. Without the help of your friend and colleague, F., who took charge when I was unable to, you wouldn't have had such a graceful and dignified burial. Without the efforts of my friends, M.L. and A., and the profuse contributions of food from various other friends, there would have been no reception at the house afterwards. And without the many who stayed faithful over the next months, the journey would have been ever so much more difficult.

These friends spent the night with me when I could no longer bear my own company in that big house, and they insisted I go to theirs when even their presence in mine wasn't enough to keep the loneliness at bay. They never complained when I showed up late for dinner dates, or even when I never showed up at all, my tortured mind refusing to cling to any sort of structure. They remembered the terrible firsts. On the eve of the anniversary of your death, I came back from work to find a bouquet of flowers waiting for me – the giver herself a widow. They drove me home from work, refusing to let me walk in the cold. But perhaps their greatest help of all was their willingness to let me talk about you. They even contributed their own anecdotes from their stockpile of memories. Sometimes during these talks I would forget and use the plural pronouns: our, us, we. When this happened, they were never embarrassed by the slips, nor did they suggest that it was now time for me to use the singular pronoun.

So you see, even when rainy weather made my vegetable garden go to stalk, and even when the sun stopped shining, and even when the wind sucked the spruce logs up the chimney, I never had to bear these tribulations alone. And so tonight I say, Thank God for steadfast friends.

NOVEMBER 24 – *Monday*

I put the family picture and the graduation picture back on the wall today. Now they give me comfort.

People keep coming up to me on the street and in stores to talk about the sale of the house. "I hear you sold the house," they say, always adding, "Do you think you did the right thing?" I'm so touchy on this subject that I want to snarl, How the hell do I know if I did the right thing? Am I supposed to be clairvoyant or something? But instead I make civil responses, peppering my sentences with platitudes such as "who can say" and "only time will tell." I can't very well admit that already I'm wishing the buyer will go bankrupt or that some other monetary tragedy will befall him, so he'll ask me to rescind the purchase.

And I'm asked what I did with my furniture. When I say I gave the bulk of it up for adoption, they look at me admiringly and then somewhat shamefacedly admit they couldn't bring themselves to do such a thing. Right on the heels of this admission, though, and as if to dismiss my sacrifice, they always add, "But perhaps you weren't attached to your things like I am to mine." It makes me want to scream, *Not attached!* God in heaven, each piece I saw going out the door was like ripping my heart wide open with a jagged knife. Why do you think I couldn't sell it?

Right up there with conversations about the house and the furniture are conversations having to do with vacations other happy couples have recently taken. I want to hear about the good times of others just about as much as I want to hear that the ice age is imminent. I listen politely, but my heart keeps up its own prattle. *Shut your face! Shut your face!* it hollers. She doesn't want to hear about your second honeymoon in the Bahamas, or about your lounging on the beaches in Bermuda. Make her day. Tell her that your husband has the beginning of prostate trouble. That he is impotent. Or he is hankering for an affair. Or even that you are!

NOVEMBER 28 – *Friday*

I purchased an answering machine. It allows me to return the calls I want to return. It also makes coming back to the apartment more inviting. I love to see that blinking light, signalling that someone cares.

NOVEMBER 29 – *Saturday*

Removed my wedding ring tonight. Friends keep telling me that the custom of widows continuing to wear wedding bands went out soon after they stopped using wives as kindling for their dead husbands' biers. After I removed the band, the engagement ring looked so forlorn that I took it off as well. But then I couldn't stand my naked finger, so I wore the diamond and sapphire ring you gave me for our twenty-fourth anniversary. I went with a couple of female friends to a movie, and afterwards we stopped at a bar. I felt like Jezebel, and I was convinced everyone in the room could see my unbanded finger.

NOVEMBER 30 – *Sunday*

The last page in the journal! I'll try to fill it with positive thoughts. I'm going to list the things I can do now that I couldn't do twelve months ago. I can:

1. Drive the car. This, I think, is an interesting aside. A couple of days ago my car went missing in the shopping mall parking lot. Of course it turned up, exactly where I had ordered it to sit before I went into the store, but a male friend came by and offered to search with me. "What type of car do you have?" he asked. "A Mazda 626," I answered smartly

and proceeded to give my license plate number. Does this sound like the woman who once told a parking attendant that she was driving a Ford Chevy? Or the young bride who, when confronted with the statement, "I see you drive a Corvair Monza," replied, "Oh, do I?"

2. Search a dark basement for intruders – although I have no idea what I would do should I come upon any.

3. Cut a squash, even one with the toughest hide.

4. Fasten my own pearls.

5. Warm my own feet.

6. Change a ceiling light bulb, even when it means stacking a chair on a table to do so.

7. Sleep alone. In this I am like what Samuel Johnson said about women preachers. They are like dogs standing on their hind legs. They can do it, but not well.

8. Travel solo.

9. Talk to service people – mechanics, electricians, etc. – without feeling that "vulnerable" is stamped on my face.

10. Talk about you without choking up.

The first poinsettias came in the stores this week, and I bought one for my kitchen table. I took a sprig to your grave and anchored it in the snow next to the unweathered monument.

My memory has remained gentle with you. It has bevelled your edges and sanded your corners. It's probably a good thing you won't be coming back. You'd hate having to live up to so much sainthood.

My grief is as constant as it was a year ago, but its pitch has lowered. It no longer has the power to bring on a migraine or make me sick to my stomach. Today I recalled the colleague, the one I mentioned earlier in this journal, who, being recently widowed, asked his neighbour of six months' widowhood when the pain went away. The neighbour didn't answer because, as he said later, "All I could tell you was that it takes longer than six months, and you certainly didn't want to hear that." If I were to be asked that same question now, I, too, would refuse to answer. What comfort would it be to say, "It takes longer than a year"?

AFTERWORD

When Goose Lane Editions suggested publishing this new edition of *When Things Get Back to Normal*, I was filled with the same feeling of ambivalence and with the same sense of anxiety that I had experienced when Pottersfield Press agreed to publish it the first time around: I told myself then that it was too private for public eyes. It was so personal it would make for dull reading. It was a vulgar display of emotions. It didn't even have a happy ending. Indeed, that first time around I had so many misgivings about the journal's publication that I seriously considered buying up all the copies in every store before anyone could get a chance to purchase them. Only the cost factor prohibited me from proceeding with this method of keeping the book out of customers' hands.

I not only had no intention of publishing the journal, I had no intention of even keeping one. This came about by pure happenstance. Anne, a writer friend of mine, brought the journal to me when she came to visit me a few days after my husband's funeral. She said I should put my sorrow on paper. She was certain this act of writing would help me immensely. It would be cathartic, she said.

To me, her suggestion sounded ludicrous. But of course

I didn't tell her so, and not merely out of politeness. My reticence was also caused by the lack of energy that comes from grief, the shock of sudden death and the job of tidying up the loose ends that the dead leave behind for the living. I thought her suggestion was ludicrous because I knew beyond a doubt that nothing could help me, certainly nothing as simple and as undemanding as scribbling a few thoughts on paper. I merely thanked her for her thoughtfulness and laid the journal aside.

A few nights later, while prowling through my house, my nerves raw from the silence of the rooms and from the always startling cutting in and out of the refrigerator motor, I picked up the journal and began scribbling a few thoughts in it. It was a last ditch-effort to quiet my nerves. Before I knew it, morning had broken. From that point onwards, I wrote down my thoughts and catalogued the meaningful happenings of my days. I found great solace in doing this. I could express my pain, my anger, my fear, my uncertainties without running the risk of having others think ill of me, without selfishly passing on to others what was clearly my own cross to bear.

I continued writing in my journal throughout the year, and by the time the anniversary date came around, not only was the journal filled, but I found I had no more need of this exercise. The *firsts* were all behind me – first snow, first spring, first birthday and so on – and I was by this time well into the process of mending. I stowed the journal away with the sympathy cards and letters I had received during the year.

It would have remained in this box had not another friend told a friend of hers about me and my journal keeping. This person was working on a segment on grief for the local CBC radio station. She asked me if I would share my writings. I was horrified. Of course not! I said all the things that I mentioned at the beginning of this Afterword – it was too personal, too dull, etc. She persisted. And persisted. Finally, I relented and agreed to read a five-minute section of it on her program. Immediately after my reading, which was also the end of the program, she came back into the studio. She had a certain look on her face which I misinterpreted as regret for having asked me to read. I hotly defended myself before she had a chance to say anything. "I told you it would be boring," I said. "But you insisted, against my better judgement."

Then she told me that she was astounded by the response to the reading. The studio switchboard, she said was lit up with calls asking where the journal could be purchased. My own telephone also rang non-stop all evening. This confirmed for me what I already knew from the bereavement groups I had attended: the loss of a loved one through death brings about deep and long-lasting pain, and we have a great need to share these feelings of loss and pain with kindred others.

From this point and with a willing publisher, I was easily persuaded to have the journal go forth as the book *When Things Get Back to Normal*. Only later, when I was two years a widow and had struggled over the highest hump of grief, did it appear in the bookstores, and I was conflicted over my decision to have it made public. The part of me that was still wounded wanted to share my journey with those others who were still trudging through that mountain of grief. The part of me that had healed wanted to buy up all the books in the stores and hide them under my bed. I'm convinced that if money had not been a factor, I would have done just that.

Very shortly after *When Things Get Back to Normal* appeared on the bookstore shelves, I was inundated with telephone calls. It seemed that readers, having read the book, needed to talk to me – to thank me for having written it, to commiserate with me. Mostly, though, they wanted my assurance that one day, they, too, would arrive at the place where I now was. The calls were not merely local ones; they came from all over this country and from many parts of the United States as well, even though my publisher had not placed the book in the stores in the United States. As someone pointed out, I had given the book a body, but it had grown legs all on its own.

If this were a fairy tale instead of an account of a real walk through grief, I would now be telling you that in the course of time I had kissed a frog who turned into a prince and who carried me off to a magic kingdom where I began living happily ever after. However, real life has a different outcome, and besides, having been born under the sign of fastidious Virgo, I could never be induced to kiss a slithery frog, no matter what opportunities lay beyond that kiss.

And if this were a fairy tale, I would also be telling you that sorrow and grief and loss are easily put behind you. There is a candy advertisement that says you can't rush a turtle. Neither can you rush grief. It takes its own good time. Even now, fifteen years later, I can still be catapulted back into the realm of that first excruciatingly pain-filled year. It may be a soft wind, the scent of a flower, waking from a dream, the glimpse of a person in a crowd, or a snippet of a song. However, the pain no longer lingers, and after a moment's stumble into sadness, I can move on with my day.

I did quit my teaching job earlier than planned. I took this step in order to devote my full time to writing. My husband's premature death made me realize how fragile life really is and that one should not postpone fulfilling one's dream until life is tidied up and in order. "Someday" so very quickly turns into never. I now have five novels on the bookstore shelves. As well, I have a film optioned.

If my husband were to return now, he would see an amazing change in me. I have become once more a complete person, but I am convinced that he was complete enough in himself not to be jealous of this change in me. Indeed, I am certain he would be proud of me. He might even relish this change. With my new and different completeness has come understanding, and out of my pain has come compassion, and out of my struggle to climb over the top of grief has come independence. If he were to come back, I'm certain I would be a more nurturing and helpful partner to him. I regret that I wasn't then all that I could have been.

In the beginning, at the time of early widowhood, I was convinced I had lost my identity, and to an extent that was true. But through the process of growth and change, I have gained another identity. To be sure, it is different from the old one, but it is equally whole and satisfying.

I'll end this Afterword with lines from the poem "Lament," by Edna St. Vincent Millay. The poem spoke very strongly to me in the early days of my grief. Indeed, it still speaks strongly to me, even though I now have the answer to the "why" in the poem.

> *Life must go on,*
> *And the dead be forgotten;*
> *Life must go on,*
> *Though good men die;*
> *Anne, eat your breakfast;*
> *Dan, take your medicine;*
> *Life must go on;*
> *I just forget why.*